Awakening the
Principles and Processes in

Awakening the Will

Principles and Processes
in Adult Learning

Coenraad van Houten

TEMPLE LODGE

Translated by Marianne Krampe

Temple Lodge Publishing
Hillside House, The Square
Forest Row, RH18 5ES

www.templelodge.com

This edition published by Temple Lodge in association with New Adult
Learning Movement 1999
Reprinted 2003, 2011
First English edition published by Adult Learning Network 1995

Originally published in German under the title *Erwachsenenbildung als
Willenserweckung* by Verlag Freies Geistesleben, Stuttgart 1993

© Verlag Freies Geistesleben 1993
This translation © Coenraad van Houten 1995

The moral right of the translator has been asserted under the Copyright,
Designs and Patents Act, 1988

A catalogue record for this book is available from the British Library

ISBN 978 1 902636 11 5

Cover by S. Gulbekian. Cover painting by Anne Stockton
Typeset by DP Photosetting, Aylesbury, Bucks.
Printed and bound in Great Britain by 4edge Limited, Essex

Contents

Part Three: Practical Applications

Foreword

The present book is the fruit of twenty-one years of work in adult education at the Centre for Social Development, Emerson College (England), and of giving courses and lectures in many countries of the world. The experience gained in this way has been summarized here and thus made available to others.

As early as 1980, a four-week course in Adult Education was offered, based on the ideas described in this book. This was repeated annually for some time. Most of the participants were people who were only just preparing themselves to be adult educators, because, initially, the experience was that those who were already working in adult education did not like being educated!

In Germany, in recent years, the demand for the one-week course 'Adult Education as an Awakening of the Will' has constantly increased. The participants, mostly educators themselves, often urged that the new concepts and methods presented there should also be written down. However, I knew that I clearly preferred giving courses to writing books and had no experience as an author.

Yet, the demand was there, and so I started to write down everything, doggedly by hand in German, because I feared that, if I would dictate, I would become too much of a lecturer. Meanwhile, my English-speaking friends began to ask for a translation. So the book was translated, rewritten with corrections and additions, and the language considerably 'Anglicised' and revised by the Editor for the English-language edition, Paul Rubens, without whom I could not have done it. So, in this way the book came about—laboriously written by hand and revised in two languages that are not my mother tongues.

Since the development of new concepts, principles, methods and learning processes was quickly advancing while the book was being written, and since I kept discovering new elements, my impression is that many aspects are unfinished, incomplete and not explained sufficiently. May the kind reader forgive me and remember that anything that is inadequate and unfinished can have an educational effect, challenging us to correct, improve and further develop it. This is what I hope will happen with this book.

Who were my teachers? First of all, my students, the participants, who kept educating me. Their responses and evaluations were valuable learning material. Secondly, my immediate colleagues, who, in the way we worked together, were excellent adult educators for me. Thirdly, for many years there were international conferences on adult education which, with their lectures, talks and exchange of experience were an important source of inspiration. Finally, but not in any way of lesser importance, I found that studying Rudolf Steiner's way of managing his more professional courses yielded great riches. There were so many fundamental principles and methods to be discovered in them by careful research. I would like to thank all these people very much for having contributed such a great deal to my own education in this field.

What is the purpose of this book? It is based on the conviction that adult education in a new form is on the way to becoming an independent profession and, as such, has a right to exist. Also, the demand for adult development and therefore the need for real adult education will constantly increase. In industrial and other organizations this need had long been felt, but since there was hardly any good education for adult educators to be found there, it had to be brought in from somewhere else.

However, this new profession needs a conceptual and methodical basis, as well as a much deeper understanding of the Adult Learning Process as opposed to the way the child learns. It seemed to me that the present teaching of adults tends to perpetuate the way of learning that is characteristic of that for children and adolescents. This made it difficult for a true adult education to emerge.

Therefore, the present book strives to provide a basis for a new adult education profession in its own right. I am well aware, however, that this is only an incomplete beginning. May the book be a help and a stimulus for many people in this new profession. May it support adults in their attempt to deepen and improve their independent learning processes.

Although the three paths of learning that are mentioned in this book are seen as an integrated whole, this book is concerned primarily with the first of these: the adult aspect of School, or Earthly Learning. A second volume is planned that will deal with the other two: the seven Processes in both Destiny Learning* and the Path of Spiritual Research.

Coenraad van Houten
Forest Row, East Sussex, England. June, 1995

---

* Since published in German as *Ewachsenenbildung als Schicksalspraxis*, Verlag Freies Geistesleben, Stuttgart 1998. English translation forthcoming, Temple Lodge Publishing.

Introduction

A diagnosis of today's social life can give us an insight into the state of our education system, as well as of adult education. In what follows, just some of the symptoms are mentioned:

— Vocational education courses exert a highly conditioning influence; a case in point is the 'professional deformation' which many people experience in their work situations but which often does not manifest until much later. This means that the course is so structured and presented that often the individual is lost and becomes merely a representative of the profession.
— Everywhere people experience a decline in their faculty of independent judgement; there is either senseless criticism or blind trust in authority. The authority of science, for example, is still asserting itself.
— In teaching, the *human being* as such is being increasingly ignored. This results, amongst other things, in a merely passive taking-in.
— It may be observed that undigested personal inner problems are increasingly projected outwards.
— The one-sided specialization that is taking place has many unfavourable social and personal side effects.

An arbitrary additional number of symptoms could be added to this list. Also, we may read about such symptoms and their causes in many critical cultural reviews. Here, however, we are not interested in criticizing our culture, but in an up-to-date system of adult education.

One up-to-date educational system for children and adolescents up to the age of eighteen is the world-wide Waldorf, or Steiner, School Movement. It is a product of the twentieth century. However, despite the beginnings that have been made everywhere, a truly relevant contemporary *adult* education system is still waiting for its breakthrough. This may not reveal itself fully until the twenty-first century.

This demand for an adult education and vocational education appropriate to our times was made early on. Already in his *Collected Essays*,[1] Rudolf Steiner frequently commented on the necessary reform of the university system. Right back then, the demand for an independent university education was being discussed. The indications that Steiner wrote then sound very modern, and it is surprising to find how few of them have been realized at the end of the twentieth century. Just some are mentioned briefly:

— Any teaching has to be filled with the spirit of our present time. Even history and past events must be presented from the present point of view. Vocational education has to be practice- and life-oriented.

— The aim of the educators cannot be to impart their *own* views to the students. This has to be replaced by a way of teaching that develops the students' power of *independent judgement* and awakens their *own faculties* instead of presenting them with fixed beliefs.

— The large number of lectures could be reduced considerably if adult educators were to limit themselves to lecturing on those aspects about which the students cannot read themselves in the numerous (specialized) reference books. The lecturer should present many leading points-of-view so that the students can acquire a personal orientation to the topic.

— Insisting too rigidly on fixed methods of working impedes any free spirits in the development of their individuality. In assessment, for example, the focus should be on what the students are *able to achieve;* not on whether they are good at examinations, nor on the *number of hours* of lectures or practical sessions they have attended.

— The duration of the course of studies should not be orientated to the achievements of the *average* student. Many can achieve in one or two years what might take others five.

— What is very dangerous is to organize higher education

(the university system) according to the pattern of childhood and adolescent education. The former's aims of education are fundamentally different from the latter's. The aim of the regular school is no less than to help children and adolescents become human beings in the best sense of the word. It has to educate the child to become a human being. The universities (or adult education), on the other hand, have to do justice to two points of view. Firstly, it is the vocational or the technical education that is in the fore—with every science having its own method of teaching. This means that there must not be a *general* university pedagogy. Secondly, people who have been trained for a profession go into practical life where they will occupy a social position. This leads to the task of giving the students an appropriate general human education alongside their vocational education. The university has to make its students into bearers of present-day culture.

— This means that establishing a university that does justice to both aspects becomes the cardinal question of a true university pedagogy. This requires an undifferentiated university for all professions (the sciences and the arts)—a 'unified school' that, as a microcosm, will be a picture of our present-day culture. The university pedagogy developed for this purpose will be fundamentally different from all education for the lower schools.

In his essay 'University and Public Life'[1] Rudolf Steiner further developed and explained these thoughts. Asking ourselves whether, almost one hundred years later, these demands have been approximately realized, it has to be admitted with disappointment that the tendencies are going in quite a different direction.

More and more a process of selection and premature specialization is taking place at our universities, instead of developing what is generally human. Universities are not uniform places of education, but mostly self-contained faculties. They give little sign of the kind of general education of the human being that would further our culture. Sociologists have ascertained that, at the universities, students' independent judgement is decreasing, while being influenced from outside is increasing. Also, it must be noted that the courses of study take ever longer, are purely technical, etc.

The world-wide revolution of students in the sixties showed that something in the university system was utterly wrong. University professors were accused of being 'professional idiots'. A way of teaching treating the sciences as value-free, despite the devastating social effects of scientific discoveries, was strongly condemned. Whoever was working with students in those years, as this author was in Tübingen, soon noticed the so-called 'university neurosis' in most of them. A strong aversion to, even hatred of, what the university was doing to them became apparent after a few exercises.

It is true that the decrease in free, independent judgement and the influence exerted on public opinion may also be attributed to the influence of the media. It is just as true, however, that an adult education system that is in harmony with life and culture would long since have found the appropriate forms of learning that would counteract this tendency, and cultivate the kind of free spiritual life needed in our times.

To give an example, two professors will be quoted who impressed the author very much. One of these, a professor of civil law, told him that, for many years, he would teach his students everything in theory and practice they needed to know to practise their profession. During all those years the image of the human being underlying this system of law was never questioned but simply accepted. No wonder, he said, that we produce 'highly conditioned' lawyers and judges who never learned to question their own (often hidden) view of what is human.

Another professor, Dean of a university of technology, said that often he had to give a diploma to engineers because they had passed their examinations, although he was convinced that they were not true engineers. Asked what he meant by 'true engineers' he talked about the cultural and social responsibility that people should have who are leading figures in scientific research and technology. He went on to say that they were not in any way being prepared in their education to carry such responsibility. Many rise to leading positions without ever having learned to lead their contemporaries in a way that is in keeping with our times. This means that here, too, there is a lack of general human education.

There are innumerable further examples to illustrate the state of the present-day adult education system. The cardinal demand for an adult education system in keeping with our times is still unfulfilled—a new adult education conceived of as a profession in its own right.

The first part of this book will present some basic principles that may be applied in many different ways. According to need, the reader could focus more on some of these basic principles and less on others. The aim of the author was not to give a complete list of principles. On the contrary, he hopes that in the future many more principles will be found.

The second part deals with forms of learning in particular. Here, too, there is an immediate need for adult education to find new paths. Most likely we have only just made a beginning. Even now, many ways of teaching are being developed outside established educational institutions, as in-service courses, or in the framework of certain projects geared to this purpose.

The third part describes some forms of application as well as specific subjects. Chapter 15, on the schooling of adult educators, should be worked out much more. This will be a task for the future.

A word must be said about the frequent use of the terms 'adult education' and 'adult educator'. In some countries, a differentiation is made between 'adult education' and 'tertiary education'. The former means a continuing education for adults beyond school, and the latter being applied to training for a profession. Here, the terms used are meant to embrace both meanings and apply to all education for adults, whether professional training or not.

Part One:
Six Main Principles

1. Adult Learning as an Awakening of the Will

Any education has at least more or less well defined specific aims. In this book, however, an attempt is made to describe some basic principles that may play a part in any kind of adult education.

While it is true that every educational programme will take a slightly different direction, all of these basic principles are valid. All of them are based on the fact that adult education may be regarded as an awakening of the will.

Let us begin with a few thoughts on the general objectives of modern adult education.

1.1. Aims of Adult Learning

Learning, developing, changing—all belong together and are three aspects of a process constituting humanity's lifelong striving to become true human beings. This is a process that never happens spontaneously but always needs to be rekindled deliberately.

During a conference of adult educators meeting annually to research basic principles of adult education, some of the questions raised were the following: What really are we doing when we educate adults? Are we teachers teaching students, conveyors of knowledge, lecturers, companions on a path of education, adult educators, scholars? What are we? Each of these terms is already outdated and lacks the true essence of adult education. Suddenly somebody said the following words which became something like a guiding motto: 'Really what educators are doing is—awakening the will!'

Learning always means to overcome resistances, to make an effort. When adults are learning, their independent will must be involved as well. The educator has to be an 'artist of the will'. The teaching of content is important as well, both to educate the feeling life and to discipline the will life. Yet, what is most important is to awaken people's independent will—more specifically, the will to learn.

This 'independent' will to learn is connected with the nature of the human ego that is related to the will. F.W. Zeylmans van Emmichoven has described two characteristics of the human ego: it is relentless and inexhaustible. Rudolf Steiner characterised the ego as the 'working will'. To begin with, however, the will manifests as a life force or energy bound up with the body. Connecting the ego with this fundamentally, biologically bound will seems to be difficult. How can the two be brought together when teaching adults?

The connection between ego and will lives in the element of warmth. There is a physical warmth element accompanying any physical activity. There is also an original, spiritual warmth that comes about when the ego generates enthusiasm for something that is beautiful, valuable, true, good, interesting and so forth. So the ego lives *in* the warmth but also *produces* warmth. It is a youthful warmth that is created by ego activity; it is a product of enthusiasm. If this enthusiasm leads to activity, then the ego and the will combine. Becoming active for something that really fills a person with enthusiasm is already an awakening of the will!

As we shall see in Chapter 5, an essential part of the Learning Process consists in activating the 'warmth process'.

In our learning, we are supported by three drives that stir in every human being, mostly rather unconsciously, as biologically bound will. These are: the *drive for knowledge*, the *drive for development*, and the *drive for improvement*.

The *drive for knowledge* is the most conscious one. The world appears to us as a riddle, alien and unknown. To liberate us from this feeling of isolation, we need to build a bridge that will help us to understand the world and ourselves. At first, eternal dissatisfaction seems to be our fate, then the thirst for knowledge begins to stir within us, never to leave us again. Rudolf Steiner once described it in the following way: Gaining knowledge means continually to grow into that which is the whole foundation of the world. In other words, it is a continual process based on the drive for knowledge.

The *drive for development* is a basic force of the soul that constantly shapes and re-shapes it. Through polarity, development, and metamorphosis human beings live through the phases of their biography. This means that at the age of 45, for instance, we learn in a way that is different from when we are 25. This will to develop, constantly to change, lives as a driving force in the Learning Process.

Lastly but still importantly, the *drive for improvement* is the most hidden one. It definitely does exist, however. It is the sense that everything could be done better. There is no such thing as the perfect action. Everything is imperfect. Deep within us we know that we are always on the path, that we are very far from having developed the full potential of our humanness. Often, when looking back on our deeds, we feel that everything could have been done better and we will be able to improve the next time.

Educators, now, are faced with the question of how to awaken these three drives in the human being. This will be their main task, and it requires a teaching method that awakens the student's independent will to learn; a will that is constantly being fed by these three basic drives. Chapter 13, 'Learning How to Learn' looks into this in more detail.

These three, however, are also connected with the second aim of adult education. Characteristic of adults is their independence, inner autonomy and original way of acting; all nourished by their own *independent judgement*.

It would be appropriate to take a close look at our educational institutions and teaching practices with the question: has our teaching developed and furthered the independent faculty of judgement in the students? Alternatively, were conceptual models, methods, skills, etc., firmly implanted into them, which later led to the well-known phenomenon of professional deformation?

The independent faculty of judgement must become the basis of adult education, but how can this be achieved? Chapter 14 will go into this in more detail.

The two main aims of *awakening of the will* and *developing independent judgement* will accompany us throughout this book. Our present age, as well as our present soul configuration, demands such objectives. A contemporary adult education has to do justice to these needs of our present times.

In all our lives there are crises, moments in which we feel we are at our wit's end. At a time like this, our thinking fails us, our feeling life is aimlessly drifting hither and thither, our will seems paralysed. We are at a loss. This feeling of helplessness, however, is the most important moment in human development. Without it we would not become active, would not begin to ask ourselves: why? and what for?

In this respect our twentieth century is a great 'educator' for adults. Everything we take for granted, every certainty, every security, are all falling away and disappearing one by one. Trust in our companion human beings, in the reliability of the government, in the honesty of humankind, even our trust in the certainty of our own thinking, is weakened. Doubt, hatred and fear are living in every soul. We can find *inner* security in ourselves only if we manage to awaken it through our own effort of will. The spirit of the times demands an awakening of the will. Therefore, it has to become the objective of any adult education to accept and promote this independent awakening of the will as a basis for any system of education.

2. The Three Learning Barriers

When we learn, we change. In learning, however, three barriers become apparent as well, which can mainly be experienced in our thinking, our feeling and our will activities. These three resistances are experienced in different ways: as an insuperable barrier, as an abyss that causes fear; as a strong feeling of antipathy or of powerlessness. These experiences are often accompanied by a feeling of inferiority, of weakness, etc. This is precisely why courage is needed—the courage to face these feelings, to look at them and recognize them for what they are. During this process we can learn that an imaginative way of looking at these feelings will lead to a far deeper understanding than an analytical-intellectual approach. Our feeling life is oriented in two directions—thinking and willing—and therefore it is important to learn how to penetrate into problematic feelings with our imaginative thinking, and how to reinforce positive feelings with the help of the will.

The real change—the essential learning—takes place in the process of overcoming these three barriers: we begin to understand or comprehend something that was incomprehensible before. The world of our feelings has become ennobled, deepened or enriched. Often, we have also acquired an ability or a skill we did not possess before.

In adult education and development we must realize that we are dealing here with three equally important principles of learning that require therefore work on all three barriers. Any adult education that over-emphasizes one of the three, will tip the person out of balance. This may lead to innumerable dangers: over-emphasis of the intellectual without the correcting relationship to practical action; the training of skills without any real understanding of their purpose or meaning; intellectualization and drilling without including the assessing, connecting, qualitative, personal element of the feeling life. All these will lead to distortions of a dubious nature, to a hardening, to a one-sidedness and to an impairment of the true, fully human process of learning.

It is vitally necessary to add this principle of working on all the three barriers to any adult education, indeed to any learning process. If this is done, the most amazing discoveries can be made.

What makes it all the more difficult to reach this balance in our work on the three barriers is that every human being tends to overemphasize one of the three. For instance, an intellectually gifted person will tend to ignore the feeling barrier and avoid practising, while a 'doer' prefers not to cope with theory. Educators, therefore, may strengthen a one-sided disposition, instead of balancing and harmonizing the learner by their way of teaching. Thus, striving for a 'balancing of the barriers' in a true adult education will have a healing effect. Indeed, continual wrestling with these three resistances will cause the highest spiritual faculties to develop. Let us now take a closer look at the three barriers themselves.

2.1. The Thinking Barrier

The thinking barrier exists between our understanding of the world and our ego. It is like a veil covering up the spiritual reality of the world. At best, our thought models can open up a part of reality for us. At the same time, however, they are covering up other realities. They are often called 'reductionist' and 'conceptual models'. In their striving to understand the world, human beings encounter ever more enigmas that may enable them to become aware of their cognitive blockages. Unfortunately, modern humanity arrogantly tries to impose its thought processes upon the world. Much has been written about this threshold of which the whole theory of knowledge gives proof. Therefore, the author will limit himself here merely to hint at approaches to overcoming the thinking barrier:

- A basic attitude to all phenomena is required that wants to question and investigate rather than passively take in knowledge.

— The learners have to understand that, instead of imposing human-made models on reality, *they* need to change so that the reality of the world can reveal its truth to them. Any belief that there is just one right idea or method—our own—is misleading.

— To school our ability to *observe* objectively with all twelve senses is just as important as developing our *thinking*; only the two combined can lead to the truth.

— We must learn to distinguish between what we *know* and what we *understand*! We must ask: what have I merely taken on, and what have I made my own? This leads to the insight that to realize the full truth the other two barriers must be crossed as well.

In practical life we find that nearly everybody experiences reality in a different way. There are people who can only deal with what is concrete. Others experience a more abstract way of working as truth. Others insist on a merely analytical or synthetic method. There are even people who find it difficult to understand anything expressed in images; to them it is a frightening, nebulous or whimsical speculation. Descriptions, they say, are not scientific. Definitions are the only things that count. Others claim that definitions are a means of covering up a lack of insight.

Due to our inclinations or upbringing we are all one-sidedly disposed to creating our own thinking barriers.

Adult educators can never satisfy everybody, simply because everybody has a different way of thinking. This, however, makes it necessary for them to become counsellors for problems arising out of the encounters at the threshold of thinking—counsellors in helping to overcome our one-sidednesses.

Firstly, they have to help the learners discover their blockages. Secondly, they have to advise on what exactly to do to overcome them. Thirdly, they must accompany them on their path of practice. During this process, the adult learners increasingly develop the ability to open up to the world (with fewer barriers), so that its truth may come to reveal itself within them (see Diagram 1).

The literature on spiritual science gives many indications on how to develop our thinking. A good example is Rudolf Steiner's lecture on *Practical Training in Thought*.[2]

For the adult today it is much more important to receive help in dealing with the barriers to thinking than simply to take in a great deal of content inadequately and passively.

2.2. The Feeling Barrier

The feeling barrier lies between the human ego and the individual's understanding of her- or himself. It is not a world-ego relationship but an ego-ego relationship. As we shall see, in the human being's actions, the will being has to do with an ego-world relationship.

Human beings want to understand themselves and, above all, their feelings. In the learning process, experiences, antipathies, sympathies, anything to do with emotions will express itself in feelings. In this process we encounter a threshold, a resistance that comes to expression in our feelings. To approach this resistance in a cognitive way, or even

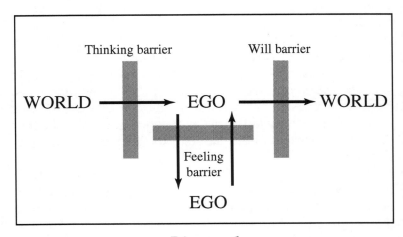

Diagram 1

with the willingness to change, seems to be particularly difficult for many people. The educator, too, seems to be very reluctant in this respect and not very inclined to consider the feeling barrier as an essential part of the learning process. In practice, we can often hear: 'That is too subjective!'; 'Too personal!'; 'Adults have to be left completely free!'; 'Invading privacy'; 'Egotistic'; 'Too intimate'; some people even use expressions such as 'unhealthy self-interest', and the like. This only shows that the educators themselves have enormous difficulties with their feeling barrier. Here, the educators are confronted with their own threshold. Yet it seems to the author that the most important, but at the same time most neglected, task of adult educators is to find a creative way to cope with this most personal feeling barrier that continuously accompanies all our learning processes.

Two basic elements of learning take place in the middle realm of feeling: the activity of the 'experiencing soul' and of the 'judging soul'. A learning process through which we do not unite ourselves in a personal, experiencing way cannot contribute to human development. Neither can a learning process that does not involve independent judgement. For a comprehensive description of the 'experiencing soul' and the 'judging soul', its origin and context, see F.W. Zeylmans van Emmichoven, *An Anthroposophical Understanding of the Human Soul.*[3] (See also Diagram 1.)

Overcoming the feeling barrier does not so much mean breaking through, as in thinking, nor is it a test of courage, as with the will. Rather, it is to do with changing ourselves. The real development takes place in our feeling life. Unacceptable feelings cannot be suppressed forcibly, but they cannot be simply lived to the full either. In neither case is there change. In the literature on adult education there is little about the learning path to self-knowledge. The literature on spiritual science, on the other hand, has much to say about inner or spiritual development, since the feeling barrier is the actual inner threshold to the spiritual world.

One of the subsidiary subjects offered in various anthroposophical courses is 'Knowledge of the Human Being'. This is helpful yet insufficient, unless it leads to personal self-knowledge. Adult educators have no way out, they have to make themselves familiar with the nature of this threshold—the threshold between our conscious and unconscious soul life—that manifests itself in all the feelings that are part of our learning process. Precisely because we are touching on the personal sphere, a friendly and understanding attitude is required that does not criticise, condemn, blame or rebuke. This, however, is possible only if adult educators, in their own feeling life, have come to a certain maturity by first having worked on 'Learning how to Learn'. Work on all three barriers will lead the learner to self-knowledge. Increased understanding of oneself is a basic ingredient of Adult Learning.

Some possible approaches are:

— Anyone involved in the Adult Learning Process has to understand how important it is to attend to the never-ending emotional resistances in a constructive, learning way. Any stirring of emotions that is not superficial is important and essential, and has something to say. It needs to be taken seriously and examined, until the 'message' that wants to come to the surface can be integrated into the learning process.

— A thorough understanding of the stages of our bio-graphical development is helpful, as is a conception of the way our soul develops from crisis to crisis. This includes learning through our feelings. This is essential in achieving a learning process that involves the full personality.

— The educator must be able to have 'helping conversations'. With these, the most important quality is true, perceptive listening. The schooling of the adult educator must include the practice of the 'helping conversation.' In many places of education the students keep complaining that they simply cannot find anybody with whom to have a personal conversation. However, adult students must also learn to conduct this kind of conversation. In using the term 'helping conversations', the author wishes to emphasize that he does not mean psychotherapy.

— Some courage is needed to enter this delicate area. Experience has shown that beneath this feeling threshold a great deal is hiding that is embarrassing and difficult, but unexpectedly beautiful and positive as well. Working on the threshold of feeling usually brings liberation and a degree of inner maturity.

— The experience that our feeling life itself may become a faculty for knowledge and understanding ought to kindle the desire in us to go through this education of our feeling life.

— It must be emphasized again that these approaches apply both to the educator and the adult learner.

2.3. The Will Barrier

As already indicated, the will barrier has to do with the relationship between the ego and the world. The ego wants to do something in the world; it wants to form, reshape, organize, achieve something. In doing so it meets with a resistance in the will region.

It is true that there are many people who learn by doing, who 'gain insight by actively dealing with the world' (Rudolf Steiner), who go on a so-called path of discovery or prefer an experimental way of proceeding. Yet many educators have observed that people's will is often paralysed at this threshold.

They still take in new things or engage in activities, but these are activities presented to them and are typical of our technological age. These actions must not be confused with 'being active', for they exclude a conscious directing by the ego that, consequently, diminishes the ability to take hold of the will itself. Rather, in our times, these regulated actions indicate a laming of the will life. This prevents us from *actively* dealing with the resistances in the realms of thinking, feeling and will. We tend to become conditioned learners instead of independent adult learners.

The fundamental character of this resistance in the will is the force of fear; a fear that remains somewhat hidden. It is a fear that lives in our will which expresses itself as an anxiety in our feeling life and an uncertainty in our intellectual life. A complaint frequently heard in adult educational institutions is that the students' will to learn is too weak, that they have too little stamina, give up too quickly, prefer to avoid difficulties, remain passive onlookers; that they are unable to commit themselves, will do only what is emotionally pleasant, and so on.

Fear is the root cause of all this, and it is increasing more and more. In the past it used to be a fear of death that would paralyse people; today it is a fear of life and a looming fear of the future. Finally, the fear of destructive forces in oneself is becoming increasingly apparent and can become the strongest influence.

The main problem in the will region is therefore the courage to learn, change and develop. Thus, the main task of the adult educator is to become an awakener of people's will, to assist them in transforming fear into courage. The deepseated and manifold phenomenon of fear should become the educator of courage.

We can mention in passing that with the customary education of skills involving practising that is prescribed in every detail, this fear will not emerge; it is covered up. However, it will certainly make itself felt as soon as an independent decision is required. This explains why, in many places of education, there is a tendency to build in outer securities and organize prescribed learning processes planned in every detail. It is obvious that, here, human beings are being determined from outside and that their will is not being awakened.

Here are some more indications on how to awaken the independent will to learn:

— Artistic activities can be very effective, since they speak to the formative, creative element in people that unites the soul with sound, colour, word, movement, etc.

— Often it has been observed that, particularly in learning groups, group work, too, creates a strong commitment. Often, the group is more successful in bringing the will into movement than one person working alone.

— Good results have been achieved with project work as a learning method.

— The structure of the learning process itself also affects the human will: presentations only of content call forth antipathy; the subjective, the personal element, has an involving effect. The structure of the learning process, on the other hand, can affect the will. This is why it is important in longer courses to pay particular attention to the structure of the learning process.

Chapter 8 goes into these four indications in more detail.

Thus, we can say that one of the main concerns of adult education should be to give equal recognition to the three resistances to learning, to bring them into balance and give the students concrete assistance in overcoming them. Another way of putting it would be: Adult education must address the whole human being in the process of learning.

Let us conclude this chapter with a little exercise. Ask yourself what the resistances are that you encounter when learning? Which are the strongest and which are the weakest impediments in your *mental* processes; in your *feeling* life; your *will* activity? Are these strengths and weaknesses a *natural* disposition, *conditioned* into you, or have they *emerged* as specific responses to life experiences?

After the following chapter it will be even easier to answer the second question. Working on these two questions we can get much information about our way of learning.

3. The Three Paths of Learning

A detailed examination of how and where in human life learning takes place, will make us discover three very different *areas* of learning and, as we shall see, also three different *paths*. The term 'Adult Learning' is used here in connection with each of the different learning paths.

The most well known of the three areas is the organized learning situation. This is characterized by the presence of a teacher, a learning objective and a particular pre-planned course that is to help the student reach the learning goal. This, applied to work with adults, is School, or Earthly Learning, or Adult Education. However, asking oneself whether this is the only form of learning, we will make the surprising discovery that human learning largely takes place outside the classroom, seemingly unplanned, without any goal and without a teacher. Often in life, we find ourselves in circumstances to which we have to do justice. They challenge us and we have to cope with them. Many people say that life is the best teacher, or that destiny confronts us with trials that, in overcoming them, help us develop new skills, a considerable human maturity or gain deep new insights. Let us call this second area of learning 'Learning through Life' or 'Destiny Learning'.

Then, there is a third area of learning which is not quite as obvious as the other two, but which has always been there and which is becoming increasingly important today. It is the inner Spiritual Schooling Path. It can unfold faculties in us that enable us to understand and enter the spiritual world. This means, to live and do research in the higher worlds beyond the threshold of normal day consciousness. In past cultures of humanity, this always used to be the most important path of learning. For reasons of brevity, the three paths of learning shall be called hereafter:

— 'School Learning', 'Earthly Learning', 'Adult Education', which can lead to 'Adult Learning';

— 'Destiny Learning', or 'Learning through Life';
— 'Spiritual Schooling Path', or 'Path of Spiritual Research'.

3.1. School, or Earthly Learning

As already mentioned, School Learning takes place within a structured learning situation: at universities, technical colleges, in lecture rooms, classrooms in any other educational institution; even at work, people often meet with brief learning situations. An organized learning situation is created. A course takes place that is divided into classes, lessons, in days, weeks, months, years. In other words, it is a consciously planned process of learning over time. Be it totally free or rigidly structured, there will always be a time schedule for the course.
Briefly:

— A course, a learning process, takes place over time. This learning process is conducted by a faculty of educators, who are considered to be qualified to teach adults.
— School Learning is imparted by teachers. The learning objectives are extremely varied: the sciences, the arts, specific technical trainings, general education, short courses that are to train specific skills, and so on. In other words, there is always a learning objective; otherwise the whole process is pointless.
— *School Learning has a consciously given learning objective.*

3.2. Destiny Learning or Learning through Life

How, then, does Destiny Learning take place?

— The learning situation is life itself, seemingly unorganized, accidental, arbitrary. Everyone is constantly faced with a discrepancy between their inner faculties, strengths and weaknesses, on the one hand, and what comes towards them as necessities, questions, challenges of life, on the other. This is the situation of their 'Destiny Learning'.

If every evening we look back on what we have been able to learn that day, we notice how incredibly instructive this 'Learning through Life' may be.

— Studying biographies can be a very appropriate method to understand the course of Destiny Learning: What life theme runs through the biography? What problem repeats itself? What are the strengths in us to which we owe the happy and unhappy circumstances we have gone through? Who are the people that have contributed to our development, both consciously, and unconsciously?

Asking these questions will give us an idea of the 'education course' of life. At the same time we will find that this course about the destiny of life holds a deep wisdom. Learning to perceive the composition of a human biography as a learning process can fill every adult educator with deep awe and admiration. It reveals itself as a divine piece of art, and may serve as an archetype for the design of all courses.

— This leads us to the question of who is the adult educator in this Destiny Learning. If we regard destiny as something that has its origins in many previous lives, we may come to the conclusion that it is a process of learning that has a deep connection with our own development as a human being. Our present life is then only the next step, so to say. It is how we encounter the questions of destiny that institutes today's process of learning. We may, therefore, speak of a self-conducted learning process. However, the learning circumstances of the future will depend on how we accomplish this present path of learning. Thus, taking this Destiny Learning into their own hands will become the main task for adults in their process of 'Learning how to Learn from Life'. The question remains: Who has composed this wonderful network of destiny? To answer this question, we have to investigate closely, through spiritual science, the whole path that is taken from death to a new birth. In the course of this path, the previous life is reviewed and the new destiny for the future life is composed in concert with all those divine beings who contribute to the shaping of our destiny. Through this investigation the adult educator may learn much about the 'didactics of the gods', which could give an increasing number of impulses and insights into the mysteries of adult education.

— The objective of this Learning through Life or Destiny is human development as such. Its means are karma and reincarnation.

3.3. The Spiritual Schooling Path

— Where, on the Spiritual Schooling Path, is the learning situation? It is, generally, an exceptional state, totally separated from outer influences, dedicated to our inner life. An important part of this Schooling Path consists in developing the forces we need to bring about this exceptional state at will. Instructions on how to develop these forces have frequently been given in the literature of spiritual science. The main thing is that we have to do it ourselves.

Concentration, inner quietness and a specific basic mood have to be created to prepare the conditions within our soul that are needed for this learning to take place. Our own soul becomes the classroom, the learning situation.

— There are also other courses of instruction for the Spiritual Schooling Path, which, however, are quite different for the very different paths of initiation (that is, the oriental, western, southern and even northern paths). In ancient times initiation took place in mystery centres. This is where the 'apprentices' went to undergo the course of their Schooling Path. One of the last places where this took place was the School of Chartres in the late Middle Ages.

Due to today's individualization there are as many different paths as there are people; and yet there are certain basic characteristics to the modern Schooling Path. 'Modern' here designates a Spiritual Schooling Path that is appropriate to the present stage of development of humanity, or even leading beyond it. Thus, on a modern Schooling Path, the person's independent judgement is increased with each step. Self-knowledge is a necessary prerequisite to pre-empt illusions.

The teacher or educator has the function only of an adviser; 'obedience' is not demanded. The starting point is the attitude that is held by some modern scientists who will accept only what they have understood. At the same time, they will not reject what they have not penetrated yet with the mind. All of these are qualities that a healthy modern adult education should indeed foster.

— Who does the teaching on the Spiritual Schooling Path? Firstly, it is the published literature of spiritual science, for it gives detailed information about this path. Additionally, experienced people may counsel the person treading the Schooling Path. The relationship is similar to that of asking advice from an expert in a certain field. The relationship on both sides remains absolutely free. Everyone finds their teacher within themselves. To pursue a Spiritual Schooling Path means to step over the threshold between the normal day consciousness of physical sense-impressions and supersensible spiritual consciousness. This crossing of the threshold involves the risk of numerous errors and illusions. That is why this threshold is guarded by a being called the 'Guardian of the Threshold'. This Guardian either allows the people concerned to continue over the threshold or rejects them until they have acquired the necessary strength and self-knowledge to cross it without any danger. Thus, this being becomes the guide on the Spiritual Schooling Path. Here, the advisory function of the adult educator serves the purpose of helping the learners to find their own teacher, the 'Guardian of the Threshold.'

— What is the learning objective? The highest learning objective that exists is: to become ever more a human being, to be able to experience our true being in the cosmic world of our origin. This is so that we can become better able to fulfil our tasks here on earth. Many young people are already very aware that they do not simply study a subject to pursue a science or become accomplished in an art, but to become more of a human being *through* their profession. On top of everything we must not forget that it is humanity as a whole that is already crossing over this threshold, more or less consciously. This very fact will give a new dimension to adult education, since spiritual experiences can invade our normal learning process, causing confusion, unless the path of Spiritual Schooling, and that of self-knowledge in Destiny Learning, are pursued simultaneously.

These few indications show the differences among the three paths of learning, and point out how different these three ways of learning are. The university of the future ought to include all three. This is why the basic principle of a new type of adult education should be the interpenetration of these three paths of learning so that they may fructify each other. In this way a comprehensive adult education system could emerge. The hope that this may be achieved one day has been living in many students for some time. However, the teachers capable of integrating the three paths of learning to a higher synthesis are still difficult to find, for this would require an intensive schooling of the adult educators themselves. At present, many institutions of adult education exist, but who educates the new adult educators?

3.4. The Connection between the Three Paths of Learning

School Learning could become a good preparation for the two other paths of learning if, for instance, it were to integrate questions of destiny into the teaching. By doing so the connection between what is being taught and our own destiny will then become ever clearer. Eventually this will also lead to the existential questions: What is the human being? Who am I? What is the meaning of our existence? What am I to do? What profession am I to choose? Which way should I go, and why? These are questions to which we can find answers by treading a Spiritual Schooling Path.

Studying spiritual science is still part of exoteric learning. *Internalizing* it and bringing it to *rebirth* in ourselves, is part of Destiny Learning. Researching the personal fundamental questions about ourselves and our tasks and responsibilities towards humanity and the earth is part of the third path of learning. Here, we may recognize three steps that occur one after the other and build on each other. They are three steps in awakening the human will.

3.5. The Ego and the Three Paths of Learning

There is also something that the three paths of learning have in common. Our ego, which is the central core of our being, is involved in all three learning processes. It even carries the continuity of our being. Without continuity there is no learning process. Therefore, it is the ego that connects the three paths of learning. In our daily life it is a matter of making our ego fit for the earth, able to rise to the demands of life. In doing so the ego becomes increasingly more adult, mature, capable and independent. Independent judgement is almost the greatest gift that life on earth can give us. However, it is founded on our memory. It is the memory that ensures the continuity of the earthly learning process.

Our spiritual path is the path that leads from our ordinary, earthly ego (often called 'self') to our cosmic ego, our higher ego. At this level, our ego is truly at home. In this process, earthly memory is not a help but a hindrance. At best, a notion that there is a life before birth can help us. In a way, the Spiritual Schooling Path is a reversal of 'Earthly Learning'; it is 'Heavenly Learning'. However, we must take with us the *fruit* of our earthly life, our independent judgement, so that it is not totally lost when we cross over the threshold. Destiny Learning, too, has to do with our ego. Here, it represents the continuity of our numerous earthly incarnations. The content of our ego is the 'learning result' of all past lives on earth. Our destiny leads us to experience the consequences of our deeds that were committed in previous lives on earth. As already mentioned, we, together with the higher powers of destiny, prepare our destiny between death and rebirth. Destiny, therefore, is both a Heavenly and an Earthly Learning Process; it connects heaven and earth, it is the bridge between the physical and the spiritual world. Here, earth and cosmos are working together, thus connecting our 'Earthly Learning' with our 'Spiritual Learning'.

Through this integration of the three paths of learning, adult education centres will again become places of initiation. This means that a new kind of didactics, new forms of teaching, a new profile of the adult educator, will be asked for. The dissatisfaction and rebellion of several generations of students, which has manifested repeatedly in the twentieth century, should be recognized as an indication that it is high time. Diagram 2 gives a short graphic illustration of the three paths and their connections

We might imagine that this whole process always begins with 'Earthly Learning.' It will then naturally lead on to Destiny Learning, and this again will prepare the way for the Spiritual Schooling Path, or Path of Spiritual Research. The other way round, however, is also possible. A Spiritual Schooling Path may lead to more intensive Destiny Learning, which in turn could be a very strong incentive to learn a specific profession.

The author has often worked with course participants on the three learning paths. In doing so, he found: The more the

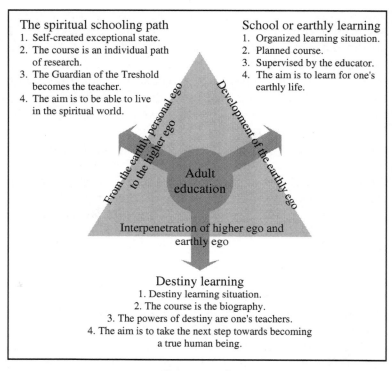

The spiritual schooling path
1. Self-created exceptional state.
2. The course is an individual path of research.
3. The Guardian of the Treshold becomes the teacher.
4. The aim is to be able to live in the spiritual world.

School or earthly learning
1. Organized learning situation.
2. Planned course.
3. Supervised by the educator.
4. The aim is to learn for one's earthly life.

Development of the earthly ego

From the earthly personal ego to the higher ego

Adult education

Interpenetration of higher ego and earthly ego

Destiny learning
1. Destiny learning situation.
2. The course is the biography.
3. The powers of destiny are one's teachers.
4. The aim is to take the next step towards becoming a true human being.

Diagram 2

participants are allowed to take part in shaping the learning process—without, of course, losing sight of the learning objectives—the more they become aware of destiny processes, individually and among themselves. The less we have previously planned and fixed the exercises and other forms of learning, the more those learning processes can come into play that are important at this moment for this particular group of participants. This, however, requires that adult educators have a large variety of teaching forms at their disposal, to be varied constantly according to the demands of the actual situation. Moreover, a great deal of courage is required to live and act in an unplanned, continuously changing human situation. The uncertainty disappears, however, when adult educators begin to experience themselves as part of the unfolding destiny situation, and to view the events as steps in their own spiritual paths. If the participants of a course were to start practising the ability to 'learn how to learn', experiencing Destiny Learning, while developing an attitude of research, the beginning of the third path of learning would have been made. Therefore, it is conceivable to structure courses in such a way that they would begin with the Schooling Path, thereby giving a totally different character to Destiny Learning and Earthly Learning. Chapter 13, 'Learning How to Learn', will go into this in further detail. Chapter 12 gives further details of the Seven Learning Processes for Destiny Learning.

4. The Image of the Human Being has to Permeate Everything

Every adult education course, just like all sciences and arts, is based on a definite image of the human being. Even a driving school has a certain image of what is a good driver. Whether this is expressed in their teaching schedule as well, is a different story!

Concerning adult education, however, the point is to shape all processes in such a way that they will make it possible for the relevant image of the human being to become alive in the participant. Many courses are not organized according to what the human being is. The human being is not seen as the golden thread, as it were, that winds through all the activities. People study pure science (value free) or an art, or a specific profession; they are trained in intellectual and/or manual skills; they learn management techniques without, however, developing the art of management as such. All of this has certain consequences, of course. Students often complain that their teachers are like professional robots and difficult to meet as human beings. Others speak of professional deformation, of conditioning, instead of development, etc. To preempt these dangers adult education institutions would have to observe some basic principles.

4.1. The Educational Situation

Over time, any educational institution will develop its own identity; something that is unique and characteristic of it. Just as every human being has a unique individuality, even to a far greater extent, so does an educational institution. From outside, it appears as the 'image' of the institution, but looked at from inside it has a very strong effect both on the staff and the students who struggle with it and are often identified with 'their' school by society. They are labelled as

'Yale or Harvard academics', 'Oxford or Cambridge graduates', 'Emersonians', 'Alanus artists', 'Järna students', 'Stuttgart eurythmists', etc.

The fundamental question here, is, of course, whether it is the task of an educational institution for adults to imprint its particular 'image', or identity, on the students. Is it not, rather, to be a means of helping people find their own individual path, so that they may become free creative personalities in their profession and/or life? The fundamental question is: is the institution a *means* or a *goal in itself?* In the following, some basic thoughts are formulated that deserve attention by institutions wanting to *serve* their students. The institution might be pictured as a threefold organism, in which the learning process is developed out of the meeting of the three members of this organism.

The first member is the *institution* itself, with its tradition, its style, its customs, its building, its structure and its strong identity. An educational institution is the manifestation of a being.

The second member is the *carrying group of people*, often called the college, the lecturers, the faculty or staff. This group will change, develop, differentiate into various groups, which makes it the living, dynamic part of the institution.

The third member is the *students, or participants*, who share a period of time with the carrying group of that particular institution. They come and go and change and develop in the process, but in what way do they change?

4.2. The Relationship between Institution and Carrying Group

Every time a new programme is designed, there is an opportunity to realize in the programme the underlying image of the human being in four steps.

The **First Step** is to find the guiding profile: What is a painter, an engineer, a eurythmist, a scientist, a businessman, a nurse, etc.? What is the specific image of the human being the course is based on? What are we striving for?

This should be formulated as clearly and simply as possible, and in keeping with the times as well. What is important is to take our time in answering these questions, for then it will be possible to take the next steps far more quickly. The **Second Step** is to select the basic principles that are most important for this particular course. These will be different for an art college than for, say, a teacher training college. With scientific and technical courses, for instance, it is particularly important to work on the three learning barriers. With art education, it is the three processes of making judgements that are most important. (See Chapter 14.) With the social sciences, such as education, psychology, sociology, etc., synchronizing the three paths of learning may be of particular importance. Each kind of technical education will have to create a different composition of the basic principles. This will give something of a basic priority structure to the course.

The **Third Step** refers to the composition of the learning path as such. How long should it be: three years, three terms, twenty evenings, three week-ends? How should the corresponding activities be shaped over time? While in the Second Step we are dealing with the basic priority structure, in the Third Step we are dealing with composition in time.

In a **Fourth Step** the actual programme is put together in detail, with timetables, teaching elements, teachers, rooms, etc. The programme is then the result and expression of the three previous steps. When a programme is being designed, the timetable is a tricky problem. It is experienced as a straitjacket. Every member of staff wants more time, different time-slots, etc. Finally, after endless compromising, the timetable resembles a bad piece of production planning in industry. The reason for this is that often the programme is put together first—far too early—without the previous steps having been dealt with sufficiently. Consequently, while the timetable rules, the image of the human being gets lost on the way, the basic structure is weakened, the course gradually becomes increasingly mechanistic. Special themes and subjects become the goal, and the totality is lost. It would be good practice to recreate the four steps once every year, working from the top, down to the final programme, so that the original image of the human being and the guiding principles of teaching may truly live in the programme.

The regular recreation of the first three steps by the carrying group will help the most important educational ideas incarnate into reality. It is a vertical process that, when neglected, may lead to outwardly perfect programmes that have nearly lost their original impulse. In teacher education, for instance, these may be a useful, practice-oriented programme; but it is an open question whether the image we strive for of the true educator still permeates everything. The reverse is possible as well, of course. In that case the First Step is very well worked out, but it remains an ideal, and is not put into practice in the actual teaching. (See also Diagram 3.)

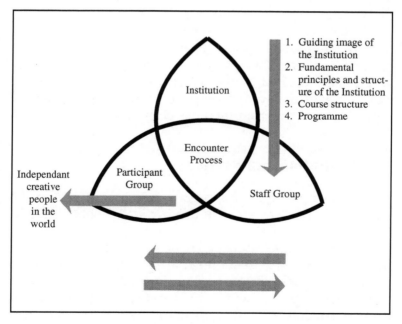

Diagram 3

4.3. The Relationship between Carrying Group and Participants

While the preparation of such a course is more like a vertical incarnation process, the relationship between teacher and participant is more a horizontal one. It is an encounter process, a relationship between adults, with both groups having much to give. Much depends on this encounter process, for it is the heart of the learning process. The way it takes place determines whether or not the participants will be able, afterwards, *independently* to put into practice what they have learned. The way we treat a child in this context is very different. The goal of child education is to help the child unfold into adulthood. Adult education is a meeting between two adults, who are co-responsible for the process of learning. In this process the mutual problem of interdependence and authority has to be solved. In Chapter 7 the reader will find more about the professional attitude of the adult educator in this respect.

All that needs to be mentioned here is that this meeting process, among other things, determines whether the guiding principles and impulses given by the school will be individualized and recreated by the participants in an independent way, or whether they will simply copy them and become a replica of what the institution has given to them.

4.4. The Relationship Between Participants, Institution and Society

The training manager of a large company once said to the author: 'For four years I went to a private school in the UK. Every day I was told that I was very privileged to be allowed to attend this school. It made me believe that I was a special person, much better than others. I have never been able to get rid of this feeling that was drummed into me. I have never, therefore, been able fully to become myself. It has also done considerable damage to my career as an educator.' There are endless varieties of this kind of story; it is one of the sources of the above-mentioned professional and social deformation. Once we have finished an education it would be good to ask oneself, looking back, whether the institution served one's *development* or whether it *shaped and formed* one according to its—often hidden—image of the human being. We must not forget that in past ages the leading schools would shape their pupils according to their spiritual aims. This was even their task. This is no longer in keeping with our times! Today we should be able to leave school with a feeling of gratitude for what the school has developed in us, so that we may freely create something new out of it.

4.5. The Relationship between Institution, Carrying Group and Participants

This is to be seen as a continuous encounter process. The aim of present-day adult education institutions should more and more be to serve the individual creative human being. In this context it is very important in what way the threefold meeting described above between *participants*, the *carrying group* and the *being of the institution* takes place. Therefore, the encounter process has been placed in the centre of Diagram 3, at the crossing of the three 'force-fields' of the institution, the carrying group and the participants. So that this three-fold meeting, that regularly needs to be cared for, takes place, the following five activities could be helpful:

— It is very important for the members of staff to be in a constant process of development, as individuals and as a group. Three to four weeks of well-prepared work by the staff, with creative discussion and co-operative research, are the source of the spiritual life of the institution. Other activities done in between also prove to be fruitful. How to take care of the relationships among the staff will be discussed separately in Chapter 15. Here, it just needs mentioning.

— It is indispensable to reconsider the overall educational objectives on a regular basis. Each institution carries the seed of its own 'death' within it, which means it is in danger of becoming traditional and stuck in its 'proven' forms of teaching. Yesterday's answers must not automatically be applied today! Education institutions should not only be contemporary, but prepare the future as well. What will be asked for by the people of the twenty-first century?

— Courses must constantly be reshaped and renewed with the help of the above-mentioned four steps. No programme, not even a lecture must be repeated without change. Everything has to be recreated every time.

— Keeping in touch with former participants, following their biographies, is a possible way of research to help shape the courses. Have the seeds grown which hopefully were planted during the former participant's 'apprenticeship'? Can we discover an independent creative attitude, or are we dealing with a faithful follower shaped by the educational institution?

— The adult relationship between staff and participants needs constantly to be looked after during the course. (See Chapter 7).

5. The Adult Learning Process

Why the human being is able to learn, and how exactly the process takes place is still a deep mystery. There are several scientific explanations, none of which, however, is fully satisfying. Learning by imitation can still be explained. It happens in the animal kingdom as well. What is far more difficult to understand is how we learn in such a way that we change, even develop into something we were not before. In other words, something happens that is more than unfolding given talents. How is it possible to let something grow that was not there before, bringing something fundamentally new into the world? This is the kind of Adult Learning we are concerned with here.

We owe to Rudolf Steiner and the Steiner Waldorf School Movement the insight that the learning of the child is based on the life-forces which, around the age of seven, are partly freed from their bodily function, thus making the learning process of the child possible. This is dealt with in further detail in the anthroposophical educational literature. It is obvious, however, that as the child becomes older this learning process changes every year, taking a considerable step during puberty. It is really only after the age of 21 that those life-forces that are no longer needed for the bodily functions become freely available to the ego. Therefore, to put it in a simplified way, Adult Learning is based on the use our ego makes of the life processes that were originally involved in the forming of our body. Our available etheric forces, energized by the ego, produce Adult Learning.

Thus, a basic principle of adult education ought to be to shape the individual learning process according to these life processes (there are seven of them) and to fashion the whole teaching process of the educator accordingly.

In the following, the author gives a brief description of the biological life processes, as well as their correlation with the learning processes.

5.1. The Seven Life Processes

A detailed description of the life processes may be found in Rudolf Steiner's lectures on *The Riddle of Humanity*.[4] The following is a quotation from the lecture of 12 August 1916. We are starting from the assumption that all learning is first taken in through the senses.

The situation of these powers of perception is different from the situation of forces that could be said to reside more deeply embedded within us. Seeing is bound up with the eyes and these constitute a particular region of a human being. Hearing is bound up with the organs of hearing, at least principally so, but it needs more besides—hearing involves much more of the organism than just the ear, which is what is normally thought of as the region of hearing. And life flows equally through each of these regions of the senses. The eye is alive, the ear is alive, that which is the foundation of all the senses is alive; the basis of touch is alive—all of it is alive. Life resides in all the senses; it flows through all the regions of the senses.

If we look more closely at this life, it also proves to be differentiated. There is not just one life process. And you must also distinguish what we have been calling the sense of life, through which we perceive our own vital state, from the subject of our present discussion. What I am talking about now is the very life that flows through us. That life also differentiates itself within us. It does so in the following manner (see next page). The twelve regions of the twelve senses are to be pictured as being static, at rest within the organism. But life pulsates through the whole organism, and this life is manifested in various ways. First of all there is breathing, a manifestation of life necessary to all living things. Every living organism must enter into a breathing relationship with the external world. Today I cannot go into the details of how this differs for animals, plants and human beings, but will only point out that every living thing must have its breathing. The breathing of human beings is perpetually being renewed by what they take in from the outer world, and this benefits all the regions associated with the senses. The sense of smell could not manifest itself—neither sight, nor the sense of tone—if the benefits of breathing did not enliven it. Thus, I must assign 'breathing' to every sense. We breathe—that is one pro-

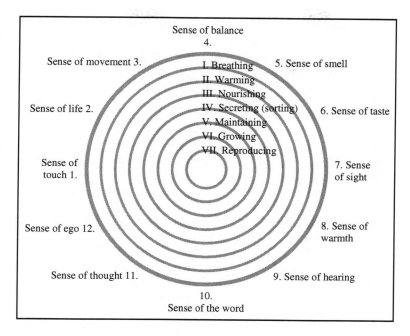

Sense of balance 4.

Sense of movement 3.

Sense of life 2.

Sense of touch 1.

Sense of ego 12.

Sense of thought 11.

I. Breathing
II. Warming
III. Nourishing
IV. Secreting (sorting)
V. Maintaining
VI. Growing
VII. Reproducing

5. Sense of smell

6. Sense of taste

7. Sense of sight

8. Sense of warmth

9. Sense of hearing

10. Sense of the word

Diagram 4

cess—but the benefits of that process of breathing flow to all the senses.

The second process we can distinguish is warming. This occurs along with breathing, but is a separate process. Warming, the inner process of warming something through, is the second of the life-sustaining processes. The third process that sustains life is nourishment. So here we have three ways in which life comes to us from without: breathing, warming, nourishing. The outer world is part of each of these. Something must be there to be breathed—in the case of humans, and also animals, that substance is air. Warming requires a certain amount of warmth in the surroundings; we interact with it. Just think how impossible it would be for you to maintain proper inner warmth if the temperature of your surroundings were much hotter or much colder. If it were one hundred degrees lower your warmth processes would cease, they would not be possible; at one hundred degrees hotter you would do more than just sweat! Similarly, we need food to nourish us as long as we are considering the life processes in their earthly aspects.

At this stage, the life processes take us deeper into the internal world. We now find processes that re-form what has been taken in from outside—processes that transform and internalise it. To characterise this re-forming, I would like to use the same expressions that we have used on previous occasions. Our scientists are not yet aware of these things and therefore have no names for them, so we must formulate our own. The purely inner process that is the basis of the re-forming of what we take in from outside us can be seen to be fourfold.

Following the process of nourishing, the first internal process is the process of secretion, of elimination. When the nourishment we have taken in is distributed to our body, this is already the process of secretion; through the process of secretion it becomes part of our organism. The process of elimination does not just work outwards, it also separates out that part of our nourishment that is to be absorbed into us. Excretion and absorption are two sides of the processes by which organs of secretion deal with our nourishment. One part of the secretion performed by organs of digestion separates out nutriments by sending them into the organism. Whatever is thus secreted into the organism must remain connected with the life processes, and this involves a further process which we will call maintaining. But for there to be life, it is not enough for what is taken in to be maintained, there also must be growth. Every living thing depends on a process of inner growth: a process of growth, taken in the widest sense. Growth processes are part of life; both nourishment and growth are part of life.

And, finally, life on earth includes reproducing the whole being; the process of growth only requires that one part produce another part. Reproduction produces the whole individual being and is a higher process than mere growth.

There are no further life processes beyond these seven. Life divides into seven definite processes. But, since they serve all twelve of the sense zones, we cannot assign definite regions to these—the seven life processes enliven all the sense zones. Therefore, when we look at the way the seven relate to the twelve we see that we have:

1. Breathing,
2. Warming,

3. Nourishing,
4. Secreting (Sorting),
5. Maintaining,
6. Growing,
7. Reproducing.

These are distinct processes, but all of them relate to each of the senses and flow through each of the senses: their relationship with the senses is a mobile one. (See Diagram 4.) The human being, the living human being, must be pictured as having twelve separate sense-zones through which a sevenfold life is pulsing, a mobile, sevenfold life. If you ascribe the signs of the zodiac to the twelve zones, then you have a picture of the macrocosm; if you ascribe a sense to each zone, you have the microcosm. If you assign a planet to each of the life processes, you have a picture of the macrocosm; as the life processes, they embody the microcosm. And the mobile life processes are related to the fixed zones of the senses in the same way that, in the macrocosm, the planets are related to the zones of the zodiac—they move unceasingly through them, they flow through them. And so you see in many ways the human being is a microcosm.'[5]

Further details about the Seven Life Processes may be found in the above-mentioned lectures.

If these Seven Life Processes are not used just for the care of the body, they can be made available to the adult ego as the basis of the learning process. They can then move in two directions:

1. They can enliven our sense activity.
2. They can transform into soul forces.

Both movements are of extreme importance to the learning process, for does not every learning process move from the outside inwards (sense activity), to appear again as something 'new', after having been internalized? The direction of the first four steps of the process is from the outside in, the direction of the last three is from the inside out. The *natural* aspect of the Seven *Life* Processes is partly transformed into the *cultural* aspect of the Seven *Learning* Processes by the activity of the ego within the learning process of the adult.

A reference is made here to the fundamental work by Christof Lindenau, *Der übende Mensch*.[6] On pages 20 to 27 he describes the thinking human being in connection with the Seven Life Processes. The attempt is made here to describe them in terms of the general learning processes, including all soul forces. With regard to the 'enlivening' of our sense activity, twelve regions of senses may be pictured that are integrated with the life processes. This is represented in Diagram 4. In the following the attempt is made to describe the transformation of life processes into learning processes.

5.2. The Seven Learning Processes

5.2.1. Breathing—Perceiving

Any learning begins with observing the world. Through the twelve senses the outside world streams into us. Only a part of it, however, which becomes the basis of the learning process, is turned into conscious observation by the ego. Something enters into us from outside. As an *organic* process it is a rhythmic breathing in and out. As a *learning* process, *attention*, at least, must be added, if anything is to be retained for the learning process itself. Only then do we *hear* a speaker, *read* a book, *perceive* sound, colour, movement, etc. Enlivening the sense activity is the prerequisite for the learning process to take place. Here, we have to pay attention to the fact that perceiving is a rhythmical process. We can take in consciously only to a limited extent; there has to be space for 'breathing out' as well. The proper 'breathing' of the learning elements is a fundamental necessity for Adult Learning. Here, too, it is important to regard this 'learning breathing' as something permeating all Seven Steps. Something is breathed in, internalized, and then breathed out again in a new form. 'Breathing', therefore, becomes a prototype of all learning—just as the rhythm of day and night carries our life through a daily breathing in of the senses and a nightly breathing out. Our whole biography, too, could be imagined as a learning process of breathing in and out.

5.2.2. Warming—Relating

For the Second Step of learning, we have to increase our inner activity to unite ourselves with what we have taken in. A relationship to the subject matter has to be established. An adaptation of our inner life takes place by way of cooling or warming. On an organic level, temperature processes continuously regulate the relationship with the outside world. This means that we stay within certain temperature limits that are in harmony with our organism. Anything that is too hot is cooled; anything that is too cool is warmed. In the learning process the ego itself has to take on this process. Being carried away by the lecturer prevents precise observation. Cooling is necessary. For boring presentations, warm interest is required to discover the essential. Every perception is tinted subjectively by approval or disapproval. Adults, now, have to learn consciously to control this feeling process, because this will increase their learning capacity considerably. In this connection, the author is reminded of something his grandfather always used to say: 'Everything is extremely interesting, provided we become sufficiently absorbed in it.'

5.2.3. Nourishing—Assimilating/Digesting

The connection between nourishing our body and nourishing our spirit is more difficult to investigate, since the bodily nourishing process is largely unconscious. In general, however, we can say that it is a kind of destruction. Tasting, chewing, swallowing, and all that takes place in the metabolic process, aims at the complete transformation of what has been eaten. To become nourishment for the body, it must be totally broken down, even dematerialized, so that it may become available for building up the body.

With our learning, if the content we take in from outside really is to contribute to our spiritual nourishment, our ego has to engage in a similar process. This means that this 'assimilation' is a rather aggressive process for which the ego activity is further increased.

Many 'digestive processes' of learning are still unconscious—as they are with children. One of the most important issues of adult education is how adults learn to break down the subject matter they have taken in and warmed, so that it may truly serve their spiritual nourishment. We shall return to this in Chapter 13.

5.2.4. Secreting (Sorting)—Individualizing

Secretion in the body determines what is to be excreted and what, transformed by inner forces, may be absorbed into the body. Similarly, in the learning process, what is useless is eliminated after assimilation has taken place, and the remainder is individualized by inner forces. Something new is born in us. 'New' here may refer to a new understanding, a new idea, a new and unexpected insight. It may, for example, become a new feeling, a value, a strong experience, or it is a new will impulse, a motivating force, a decision, etc. What is common to all of them is that it has seed character.

The purpose of the three previous Learning Steps was to create the prerequisites for a 'new birth', this means to make what we have learned really our own. It is here, in the Fourth Step, that the individualizing of the learning process takes place. 'New' does not mean that this thought, that emotion or that will impulse did not exist before, but they have been newly born in the soul of the learner. To learn means to change. Therefore, 'learning' and 'developing' are identical.

To make the 'secreting' or 'individualizing' happen, our own ego activity is required, as it were, to create out of nothing. The digesting has created the vacuum required for it. Adult education as an awakening of the will is actualized here.

It is obvious that there is much learning that takes place without digesting and individualizing. This kind of learning, however, remains peripheral. It might be called a kind of regimenting or 'conditioning', which may be of practical value for intellectual or manual skills but may also have harmful side-effects by hardening and fixing parts of our being. Therefore, the process of individualizing is the decisive kernel of adult education.

An important indication from Rudolf Steiner was that the untruthful and illusory forces of Ahriman and Lucifer are not at work in the process of secretion within the body. This is why, in Adult Learning, this sun-like space of freedom has to be lifted into consciousness. In a similar way to that of the First Step of perception, it could be said that this quality has to permeate all other steps as well.

5.2.5. Maintaining—Practising

A typical experience with learning is that we often have insights, forebodings, experiences or impulses that quickly fade away again or are forgotten. To keep them, they must be repeated. To repeat something means to practise. Thus, through regular, rhythmically repeated learning activities, the new seed is steadily incorporated into our being.

Taking care of germination demands reverence, care, a conducive environment and love for the activity of practising. Otherwise—as with the plant—the little shoot cannot thrive. For there must always be a *motivating force* behind practising: individualization; and an *aim*: developing a new faculty. If the motivating force is not present, practising may become a kind of conditioning which may result merely in intellectual or manual skills. This would prevent the growing of a new faculty. In the body, the life process of maintaining happens at night. This is through those mysterious means of regeneration by which the vitality-consuming forces of our daytime consciousness are replaced by fresh life-forces. In the learning process, we have to take care of this ourselves by doing exercises that revitalize instead of rigidify.

5.2.6. Growing—Growing Faculties

Anything living in the body dies and is renewed—in other words, it grows. The three characteristic forces of this living growth in nature are polarity, development and metamorphosis. Where, then, can we find all of this in the Adult Learning Process? The exercises as such are never a goal but a means to make a spiritual ability, or faculty, grow. This means that the outer exercise itself has to die, be forgotten, to allow something else to come about. An individual exercise by itself will rarely lead to an ability.

This is why a *configuration* of exercises with polarities, development and an overall structure brings with it the possibility of facilitating a new faculty's growth. This develops slowly, is never completed and manifests out of a metamorphosis of interconnected exercises. Growth is a musical process, a chord of exercises showing synthesis. Just as the Third Step, *assimilating,* is something of a dividing, analysing process, so *growing* shows a synthesising aspeçt. However, it is constantly transforming the concrete exercises into higher faculties.

A great deal of further research is needed before we know with certainty which composition of exercises promotes the growth of specific faculties. Otherwise we are likely just to practise and practise, and rather arbitrarily, in the hope that some time, after years, the true ability, or faculty, will arise!

The secret of growth is: every day to let the exercise die in our soul by wrestling with the resistance it presents, as well as letting it resurrect each night as a growing ability.

5.2.7. Reproducing—Creating Something New
As a life process of the body, reproducing means to 'repeat the same', that is to say a kind of multiplication. With the learning process, the point is whether we are really creating something new as a result of the previous six steps. A strengthened, or new, ability also makes an improved or new realization possible. This means also that it depends on the six previous steps whether the result will be a repetition or an original achievement. Many examination answers are a mere reproduction of what we have taken in—in other words, there has been no process of Adult Learning. This leads us to the question of what creativity is in the context of the learning process. We have already ascertained that the ego is to be creative with each of the steps. With the seventh, however, the ego does this simulta-

neously with all the other six steps, so that the result may also be more than the sum of the separate steps. This may be observed, for instance, when watching a eurythmy graduation performance, the concluding presentation of a management course, and so on.

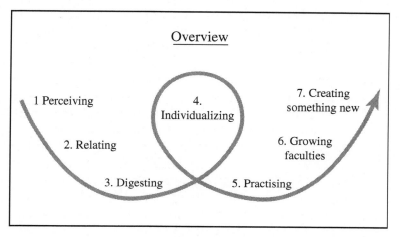

Overview

1 Perceiving

2. Relating

3. Digesting

4. Individualizing

5. Practising

6. Growing faculties

7. Creating something new

Diagram 5

— Each of the Seven Learning Processes also includes the qualities of the other six. The ego activity always produces warmth. Each step is a creative process. Always, we make use of the senses of perception. Each step involves a breathing element, etc.

— The Seven Learning Steps occur both successively and simultaneously, just as happens in the body with the life processes, although this is not always conscious.

— If one step is omitted, for instance the Fourth (individualization), the learning process is disturbed. This may, in the long run, result in damage, such as mental fixations and compulsive behaviour. Today's nervousness is caused partly by much undigested learning content remaining stuck somewhere in the human being.

— In terms of the structuring of the Seven Steps, *per-*

ceiving (1st Step) and *creating something new (7th Step)* may be regarded as a polarity, which represents a breathing in and out of the learning content. *Individualizing (4th Step)* is then the middle that constitutes the transitional moment between in-breath and out-breath. Then, too, *warming (2nd Step)* is in the middle of the first three steps, and *growth (6th Step)* in the middle of the last three. The growth of new faculties is fuelled by the youthful warmth generated by enthusiasm.

— So far, the learning process has been described as an ordered process of Seven Steps. Teaching, too, may be structured in this way. Unfortunately, the reality of human life is different. Within us there are many learning processes going on at some stage or another. Also, *taking-in (Step 1)*, *relating (Step 2)* and *assimilating (Step 3)* may happen much faster than *practising (Step 5)* and the *growing of faculties (Step 6)*. This explains the frequent 'leaps' occurring unexpectedly when learning. Therefore, the inner task of the adult learner is to harmonize the different learning processes with each other. A thorough understanding of the Seven Steps might prove helpful. This understanding of the learning processes may serve three main purposes:

1. The adult educator has to shape every programme in such a way that the Seven Processes are being supported and accompanied. (See Chapter 8.)
2. The most important thing: This understanding will help the adult learners successfully to transform for themselves even the worst education course. They then determine their own learning process. (See Chapter 13.)
3. Regarding teaching method, the adult educator ought to work in such a way that the Seven Learning Processes are awakened and promoted.

The following section deals with this question.

5.3. Didactic Aspects of the Seven Learning Processes

5.3.1. Taking in/Observing

Anything that strengthens the active use of our twelve senses will further this First Learning Step. There are already educational courses that include half an hour of observation exercises every day, which has increased the learning ability of the participants considerably. Including the senses in a proper and objective way is, however, only a first step. A second step would be to enliven the senses by way of artistic exercises, that is to say, increasingly to incorporate the life processes into the activities of the senses. A third step will then be looking through the senses, to become aware of the spiritual realities lying behind them. This is a truly Goethean way, which, however, should now become a didactic learning method, a true Schooling Path.

This will often accompany an embarrassing discovery that gives us a little more self-knowledge. For, although our senses are selfless, the way we use them is often coloured by innumerable psychological factors, and there is very little, if any, *pure* observation. Who is truly able to listen to a lecturer in an open and selfless way, or look at an art object in such a way that it may clearly express itself to us, or really to see the picture nature of another human being? Here, the fundamental attitude to be practised continually is openness, wonder, even reverence for the sense phenomena—such as young children have. The adult educators are then confronted with the pressing question of whether they are furthering or disturbing this attitude by the way they act. They may discover a great deal by observing their breathing pattern while teaching; and even more when asking the participants how their breathing rhythm responds to theirs while listening to the presentations. Due to the influences we are exposed to in our environment today, such as radio, television, film, noise, our senses have been considerably dulled. Therefore, an adult education that re-enlivens the senses is even in this way carrying out cultural therapy.

The Transition from Perceiving to Relating
The transitions always need to be accompanied didactically, since every step demands a different attitude. While the First Step is open and impartial, the Second is personal and subjective. This is because the material that has been taken in is being internalized. We unite ourselves with it, consciously bringing in our feeling life. The content of what is being taught is experienced differently by everybody. Our whole biography 'resonates' in the process. Instead of suppressing this as a disturbing factor, it is taken up and made into an entrance gate for a deeper way of learning. The adult educator has to integrate the emotions of the participants into the learning process as something valuable. In this way the First Step, of impartially taking in, is transformed into the aim of striving to integrate the different aspects of oneself in a personal way.

5.3.2. Relating
Didactically, this means: to make the process of warming possible right at the beginning, the teacher connects with the participants' world of experience. Our ego generates warmth whenever we are truly interested in something. From a didactic point of view, this requires that enthusiasm be stimulated in the participants. By showing a strong interest, both in the subject and in the participants the adult educator will promote this. Enthusiasm is catching!

In the end, however, this process of relating has to be an ego activity of the learner. Finished, logically worked-out learning content has a paralysing, antipathetic effect. Incomplete, questioning, searching processes have an activating effect. What may be useful for the learner, is to go through a lecture in the mind asking the following questions: Which were the moments when I was inwardly touched? What was important, what was unimportant? What was valuable, what not? What was sympathetic, what was antipathetic? After a while—with the support of the educator—a structure of warmth-coldness will emerge. This is a first indication of where our own essential questions are lying—with resistances being just as important as approval. Through the warm, feeling ego activity, the content taken in from outside is adjusted to our ego organization, our warmth organization. This warming humanizes the learning content. In our culture there are many forms of teaching that try to avoid, even prevent this Second Step in particular. Learning is to be taken in and repeated accurately, so that what we have learned may be reproduced again with as little effort as possible (programmed learning, etc.). However, the ego activity that should make Adult Learning into a fascinating process of discovery is weakened by just this.

To become an enthusiast the power of imagination is needed. A whole world is hidden behind the smallest, seemingly insignificant, phenomena. There are adult educators who are able to reawaken the dead intellect in a highly imaginative life by way of fairy tales, myths, and legends, as well as an imaginative way of presenting their material. Socrates put it very aptly: 'What is teaching—filling a bucket, or kindling a fire?' This process of warming has to be striven for with all possible means, because it is the fuel for the subsequent steps. Learning now must become a process of recognition, that fills the learner with enthusiasm.

To gain understanding, we have to learn to burn away by means of fiery enthusiasm anything that opposes the presented material, such as cynical, critical, mocking or hate-filled reactions. Only by burning away these reactions can we really unite ourselves with the material in order to recognize it. In the next step, that of assimilating, critical comparison, confrontation and questioning are needed, but only after we have created enough inner space for the presented material.

Therefore, the First Step is a cleansing of our twelve senses, and the second a firing-through of our inner life so that we can connect truly with the content. Of course, the Seven Processes apply equally to *any* kind of learning: intellectual, manual, artistic or otherwise.

The Transition from Relating to Digesting and Assimilating
To make this transition, the ego's drive for independence, for autonomy, has to be awakened. A fine principle in this

respect is not to *accept* anything we have not understood, nor to *reject* anything before we have truly understood it. This principle leads to constant uncertainty, because we will never understand anything completely, always only partially. The ego now has to learn to live with this constant uncertainty, replacing it by the activity of assimilating, or digesting. By their own example and constant encouragement, adult educators need to help the participants through the multiple crises of digesting the learning content, since this often needs considerable courage. It is much easier to accept everything blindly that is taught to us. Even if we are often physically very active, we are often spiritually very lazy.

5.3.3. Digesting and Assimilating

There are innumerable methods for digesting the learning content we have taken in. To mention just a few:

— *Assimilating by way of thinking*: When we read our notes, to think about them, confront them with other opinions, try to think the opposite and ask: Is there anything that is wrong, and if so where? Is it really logical, in keeping with reality? Testing the learning content with examples!

— *Assimilating by way of feeling*: Letting it resound inwardly; digesting the result of the Second Step; trying to express in an artistic way what we have taken in, then 'listening' to our feelings; letting our sense of truth speak, etc. Assimilating by way of feeling can be successful if we have already developed our feeling life, to a certain extent, into a cognitive organ, the sense of truth.

— *Assimilating by way of will*: This is the most important step since it leads to the next step, that of *individualizing*. Here, we have to confront the fundamental beliefs we have been holding so far with what we have taken in. The question to ask is not only: is this right or human? but also: is it morally justifiable from my point of view? What significance does this learning material have within the framework of my biography? Why did I not meet with it before? How does this content relate to what I am really looking for? This way of assimilating may become very existential, even leading to inner crises. It is obvious that something of all three components will flow into good assimilation, which in turn will lead to thorough digestion.

This Learning Step is really a struggle between old and new opinions, between a feeling of warmth and coldness, as well as an examination of our intentions. Therefore, this Third Step takes courage. The adult educator has to develop an 'encouraging' kind of didactic for this purpose. Artistic methods can be very supportive to such an 'encouraging' process.

The Transition from Assimilating to Individualizing
The inner struggle of assimilation must now end and be replaced by inner tranquillity, an open and listening mood. This rest period may be induced from outside by the adult educator asking for silence and quiet contemplation. However, it may also be brought about by the participants, whenever they feel that they have assimilated enough. In either case the digesting/assimilating leads to a void, a kind of 'inner open space', in which something new may come about.

5.3.4. Individualizing
Human beings really are aware of much more than they know about in their daytime consciousness. Their higher beings know, their conscience knows. In their subconscious soul-regions a large amount of wisdom is stored.

In this state of individualizing and quiet contemplation, something may break through which, having been individualized, becomes the learner's own. This break-through may manifest as a new insight, a new idea, a new understanding. Whatever we *know* becomes *understanding*, like an experience of light. However, it may also be a new way of sensing that is breaking through, a sense of value, a sense of beauty, compassion. Indeed, the whole infinite range of feelings may come to expression. Very often this individualization sets off a will impulse. An understanding becomes an intention or decision. What is decisive, however, is that these experiences are new. This is what individualizing really means. What we have taken from outside in a learning way, connected with and digested, has become truly our own.

The task of the adult educator now is to pay as much attention as possible to such experiences. These kinds of 'break-through' are happening all the time, often unnoticed, since under the influence of every-day life they evaporate quickly. To make a break-through possible and hold on to its appearance, becomes part of the teaching process. This may be done in many different ways:

— At the end of the day a learning review may be undertaken where everyone concerns themselves with the question: 'What are the essential things I have learned today, and how did this take place?' This may lead to the break-through in individual learning.

— There is a specific group process in which the participants help each other to find their individual goals. That is to say, to become aware of what their sincere, true question is. Possibly this will also lead to a process of individualizing, when it becomes obvious that nobody has exactly the same question as anybody else.

— Generally, the individualizing is reinforced when an adult educator works with questions instead of answers. Answers conclude a learning process. True questions are a beginning, have a future. From this perspective, we could say that the first three Learning Steps have been a means of making it possible to awaken the true question within ourselves. Living with a true question enhances presence of mind.

It is a good experience for successful lecturers to discover that they have started a process in another person that has very little to do with the content of their own lecture. The lecture was only a means to awaken something else in the other.

Adult education, as a process of awakening the will, becomes most prominent in the individualizing process, supported didactically by awakening the *drive to understand*, the *drive to develop*, and the *drive to improve*, as mentioned in Chapter 1.

The first four steps of the Learning Process may be regarded as a whole. They lead from the outside in, while the fourth is the starting point for the last three. See Chapter 15 for an example of how to accompany the four steps with the so-called *learning-group method*.

The Transition from Individualizing to Practising

As already mentioned, the danger of the Fourth Step is for the 'inspiration' to evaporate quickly, to be forgotten and thus lost. A first rule, therefore, is to note down this inspiration immediately, repeat it inwardly a few times, or hold on to it in another way. It is worthwhile to have a little notebook always in our pocket for, often, the 'break-through' happens when we are doing something completely different, and we must be able to make a note immediately.

The adult educator, however, has to be aware of the fact that, initially, the often brilliant ideas, experiences or will impulses, only have an inner importance for the participant. The latter still has to go a long way to be able to realize it in the outer world. This requires looking after this 'shoot' (the Fifth Step), quietly letting it grow as a new ability (the Sixth Step) until, finally, it may be placed into the world as a creative expression (the Seventh Step).

Many people have easier access to the first four steps, others more to the last three. What counts, however, is the learning process as a whole. This is what makes the transition from the fourth to the fifth process decisive.

In adult education, practising for the sake of practising, without motivation and without a clear objective, is unwholesome and even harmful. This means that the impetus, the motive, for any practising has to be the result of individualizing (Step Four). To find the most essential exercise for the new shoot becomes the first task of the adult educator. The second task is to bring about the right attitude towards practising.

5.3.5. Maintaining by Practising

If something is to be maintained, it has to be repeated— either mentally or manually. In other words, practising is the *maintaining* process of learning. In the body, maintaining occurs during the night as a kind of regenerating.

Sleeping makes it possible for spiritual beings to restore all that has been used up during the day by our consciousness. This means that the maintaining of the body should correspond with spiritual maintaining. In the learning process, this happens through practising. The question is, however, what are our exercises doing? Are they *using* up life-forces, or are they *building* up, which is generating life-forces? Are they bringing refreshment by letting new faculties grow because of these forces?

Some indications for a wholesome way of practising:

— The motive to practise must emanate from the individualizing process. Regarding the breaking-down forces, we may say: Every idea that does not become an ideal destroys a force in our soul; every idea, however, that does become an ideal within us creates life-forces within. This should become the main motivating image for all practising.

— Concerning the Spiritual Schooling Path, Rudolf Steiner often mentioned that meditation exhausts certain life-forces. They need to be restored if this practice is not to produce negative side-effects. Restoration may occur through the so-called Six Subsidiary Exercises, which have been described in various ways.[7]

This gives us an important indication:

During the learning process, practising should occur in such a way that the six activities of the Subsidiary Exercises come into play. All the exercising should be shaped in such a way by the adult educator that the basic practice of these six is included.

1. An exercise requires concentration (willing in our thinking), which means that it will not tolerate any automatic repeating of what has been done before. The practising person should be fully engaged, full of concentration and attention.
2. An element of independent activity has to be built in (thinking in our willing). That is to say, regular variations are to be stimulated. There is a very fine line between an imaginative way of practising and an arbitrary playing around. Here, imaginative direction is needed.
3. Rhythmical practising should not become mere routine nor rigorous discipline. It should be accompanied by the self-regulated feeling life.
4. Our love of practising for the sake of practising has to be rekindled repeatedly (nurturing positivity). Boredom, antipathy, an exaggerated sense of duty, etc. will again generate decaying forces.
5. The exercise should always have an element of equilibrium to it, accompanied by inner quiet. This means that there should not be anything exaggerated, or one-sided.
6. Harmony of the whole is created when the exercise has an archetypal character that involves the total human being. Experience has shown that we have to try out many exercises, many of which will be discarded again. Certain exercises, however, because they are effective and of an archetypal nature, will be retained and can be improved more and more. Spiritual beings can unite at night with exercises that are consonant with spiritual realities, thereby reinforcing and improving the exercise as well as our life-forces.

— It is important that a special environment be created for exercising. The exercise needs a home in which it may thrive; it needs to be looked after. This preparation of the physical environment and of the inner mood, to accompany the spiritual meaning, is just as important as the exercise itself. It needs to be embedded in the right environment so that this specific activity may have a wholesome effect.

This demands a great deal from the adult educator. For all these factors determine that either the practising will lead to our hardening and fixing from outside, or will become a fertile ground for new faculties. Chapter 10 describes in more detail how to design and implement exercises.

From a didactic point of view it is important to consider the three steps of digesting (Step Three), individualizing (Step Four) and practising (Step Five) as a threefold totality. Digesting and practising then become a polarity, making space for an open middle. The activity of digesting has an active, almost aggressive, male character, while practising has an intimate, caring, female character. The two of them together may give birth to something new.

The Transition from Practising to the Growing of Faculties
To accompany this transition is a never-ending task for the adult educator, since every exercise may lead either to hardening or it may become purely automatic. In other words, it could prevent a new faculty from growing. With therapeutic exercises, for instance, we may observe how it is especially the infinite variation of the exercise that has a healing effect. Therefore, when designing the exercises, the adult educator already has to bear in mind the growth process.

The difference between a skill and an ability, or faculty, is that a skill can be applied only in certain situations. It is done quite automatically and may be learned relatively quickly. Faculties, however, may be used in various ways in many different situations. Therefore, they are never totally automatic. They grow slowly and continually. In the learning process, the aim of practising is born in the individualizing process. The aim of practising is directed towards the growing of new faculties.

5.3.6. Growing Faculties

The growth of new faculties occurs in the unconscious. It might be imagined that in unconscious regions (in the night), a meeting takes place between exercises, leading to their 'marriage' and giving birth to a new ability. The adult educator is the one creating the conditions for this to happen. In doing so, the adult educator has to remember that learning always has to do with the experiencing and overcoming of resistances. Being on earth provides us with potential learning situations. When we try to become active, our will becomes dammed up in dealing with their resistances. The effort of will, however, transforms unconsciously into a new ability: of suddenly being able to do something, mentally, emotionally or manually that we could not do before.

From a didactic point of view this means that faculties can best grow in practical situations. Practising still takes place in an exceptional situation. Application in practice, however, brings many of the activities we have previously been practising and learning into a kind of synthesis. Project work, practical learning, learning through experience, etc. are didactic means for this purpose.

The last three steps, practising, growing and creating, are directed from the inside out and are more will oriented. Regarding *growing*, the 'resistance of reality' fosters the translation of these activities into an ability.

This may be the time and place to mention that many courses are too classroom-oriented, very much neglecting practice learning. However, it is also true that this kind of practice, or project, learning does require very special teaching methods on the part of the adult educator, who is often not schooled in this kind of teaching.

The Transition from Growing Faculties to Creativity
If one of the previous steps has not been done properly, the Seventh Step is in danger of becoming a mere repetition, a

summary of what we have learned, without involving a genuine new step of learning. We are talking, here, about adult education. This means that those independent adults who are endowed with an ego should put into practice in an original way what has developed in them by way of learning. It should not merely be applied as a matter of routine. The difference lies in the transition to the Seventh Step. The adult educator now has to bring about a creative attitude in the learner. Creative activity is very satisfying but may also cause much fear. From a didactic point of view, artistic activity is here the best support for the adult learners. This is not so that they become artists, but to find the creative source within themselves. As well as some specific artistic exercises, certain types of group and project work may contribute to this as well.

5.3.7. Creating

This is where the outward directed attitude finds its strongest intensification. This is because the question coming from outside has to be recognized before it can be answered in our own independent way. It is the reverse process to what has been said about the First Step of perceiving and taking in. When learning how to paint, for instance, most people are able to learn the technique and develop a sense of colour, but this does not mean that they have also discovered how a certain colour wants to be painted. In the educational preparation for socially based professions, many social forms and processes may be acquired. We may learn to observe social processes, etc., but then there is still the question of how we should and can deal with a specific social situation (which is always unique) in any given moment. Awakening the will here means to awaken the ability and activity in the learners to sense what is needed in the outside world that confronts them.

The adult educator may create many learning situations that develop this creative way of acting. Moreover, courses already exist that work specifically on developing creative faculties in the participants. In the following, this creative ability is described as an indispensable element of any process of Adult Learning.

The creative will may manifest both upwards, in the cognitive realm, and downwards, in our actions and behaviour. However, both directions originate in the rhythmic human being; in the mobile, playful, changing middle realm. The adult educator has to be aware that, somewhere, there is a creative source in everybody, but also something inhibiting these creative possibilities. The art of adult education is to find the right approach to making this source flow. An artist who is also an adult educator once told the author how the Seven Learning Processes are always active within him while he is creating a work of art.

1. We pick up an idea, for instance for a painting. It always comes from outside, but is breathed in because we are fascinated by it; it makes sense. It is artists themselves who create this perception for themselves.
2. The warming takes place as soon as we start to work, when many unexpected things happen that we have to adjust to. Artists generate the warmth that increasingly unites them to the idea.
3. Now the difficulties begin because we try to solve the problems that arise with the help of the talents we have acquired so far. Here, courage is needed really to plunge into a chaos, letting everything we know, have practised, are familiar with, fall away. Artists create an open space for themselves.
4. The open space is closed in itself, an exceptional state. It is the ego that may find its own answer in this void, not the talent. The work of art is being born.
5. This being needs to be received, loved, looked after. We must learn to handle it in a way that is appropriate to it. The artist is caring and fostering.
6. Then the being will give us the faculties it needs to manifest itself. The artist is receiving.
7. Eventually the work of art is completed, and the artist experiences that he or she has been changed in the

process. The work of art has created the artist also—a truly creative learning process.

Becoming fully aware of these Seven Learning Processes in the creation of a work of art would be the starting point from where we could put them into practice in teaching art to adult students.

In the example given above, the Third Step was the critical point, because here it was revealed whether the artist would repeat him- or herself, or create something new. With other people other steps, too, may constitute the decisive resistance.

This example may show that continual ego-activity is the prerequisite to raise the organic life processes that are bound to the body up to the spiritual learning processes. Many works of art still show traits that are bound to the body and projected outside. However, the learning processes need to be transformed fully into soul processes. Rudolf Steiner described how, regarding artistic activity, the first three processes lead to *enjoying* art, while the last four serve the *creating* of art. While being transformed into soul processes, the seven life processes unite with each other in a new way. The first three develop a kind of new thinking, the last four a kind of new willing, while the rhythm between the third and the fourth level brings about a new kind of feeling.

This is confirmed by the experiences we may have with the sevenfold process of Adult Learning. An increasingly strong artistic penetration of these learning processes will demonstrate and confirm this in the near future.

To conclude this Chapter, it should be mentioned that the path of Destiny Learning, too, may be described in seven learning processes. This will be touched on in Paragraph 5 of Chapter 12, but will be the topic of a further book.

6. The Rebirth of the Seven Liberal Arts

In many adult educators who are looking for new paths in adult education, there lives a kind of nostalgia for the wonderful School of Chartres. This had its zenith around the end of the Middle Ages, then disappeared suddenly. It is seen as the ideal education in which the seven liberal arts as seven divine virgins revealed their secrets to the pious and devoted pupil. How exactly the teaching was done is difficult to ascertain, but many writings, poems, allegories, almost mythological pictures, have been handed down. It is difficult for our modern consciousness to understand in what way the pupils were learning there, since it was really a Schooling Path into the spiritual world and had nothing to do with professional training. In tradition, however, the 'Seven Liberal Arts' live on.

The guiding model of 'the seven centres of revelation' is ancient. Many teachings were based on it, often under different names as: 'seven oracles', 'seven planetary wisdoms', in Chartres as 'seven sciences':

1. *Grammatica*; 2. *Dialectica*; 3. *Rhetorica*.
(All three together are also called the *Trivium*);
4. *Arithmetica*; 5. *Musica*; 6. *Geometrica*; 7. *Astronomia*.
(All four together are also called the *Quadrivium*.)

These seven sciences cannot at all be compared with the modern sciences because, as mentioned above, they were a Spiritual Schooling Path. There are sculptures in the Cathedral of Chartres showing human representatives associated with these individual sciences: some famous scientists, such as Pythagoras, Aristotle, Euclid. It is understandable that many adult educators regard this School of Chartres as a model and are hoping to reintegrate the Seven Liberal Arts into their teaching. Rudolf Steiner, too, seems to have mentioned that in a modern professional education the Seven Liberal Arts might reappear, albeit transformed. (As far as the author knows, this has only been handed down orally). In the outlines for a eurythmy training given by him in Stuttgart, certain features of these Seven Liberal Arts may also be seen. Therefore, the author wants to try and compare, as far as possible, what he has written about in this book with the teaching at the School of Chartres.

It will be noticed that modern humanity has a very different consciousness from the people of the late Middle Ages. Therefore, learning processes today will necessarily be very different from what they were then.

Natural sciences and their application in technology are a product of our modern times. Spiritual science gives us much enlightening information about this change of consciousness. The turning point, when humanity proceeded from the stage of the intellectual/mind soul to the stage of the consciousness soul, was at the beginning of the fifteenth century. This means, among other things, that at the time people were still able to think with their heart; thoughts were experienced with the mind, not as abstractions. The consciousness was permeated by the human being's quality as a rhythmical being of the middle sphere. Consequently, thoughts were experienced as a reality. The notion was generally accepted that sciences and arts are derived from beings who reveal themselves to the soul, if it has been sufficiently prepared by spiritual exercises that create strong feelings of reverence and devotion.

The transformation to our modern state of consciousness was extremely radical. Human beings became *head* people. (Head and nerve system are the carriers of consciousness.) Individuals acquired an awareness of things and objects, which they observed as dispassionate onlookers. This turned them into materialists. At the same time, they developed an intellect that was able to abstract from experience, and which allowed them—much more so than in the past—to become independent, individualistic human beings. What was most important for the learning process, however, was that, for the first time in history, they learned to use their twelve senses in an *objective* way for observation. It is this that created the basis for pursuing modern sciences. It might almost be said that people can now become egoists and materialists—estranged from the world and their companion human beings, but independent. Therefore, the 'apprentices of Chartres' and present-day adult students have fundamentally different dispositions.

The pupils of Chartres received their wisdom from above, revealed by teachers for whom they had deep reverence. Because of their developmental stage of the mind soul, they were able to experience this knowledge as a living being. This made it possible for them to become more and more human in a true sense. It ennobled them.

To be able truly to take in, transform and apply the subject matter, present-day students must transform the same living processes into learning instruments by exerting their individual egos. This is a learning process directed from below upwards. This allows the learners increasingly to become developing human beings, independently acquiring knowledge by their own efforts.

One of the greatest and most famous teachers of Chartres, Alanus de Insulis, used to teach that the lessons of the Divine Goddesses would enable the pupils to build a chariot in which to ascend to heaven, where they would then receive a new soul—their true soul. Only when they had achieved this were they allowed to go back to earth to teach others.

The previous Chapter described how we might, in Seven Learning Steps, develop ourselves into ever-better learning instruments. That is to say, to build vehicles with which to explore the three paths of learning (Chapter 3). By doing this, we bring those three paths steadily to a higher kind of synthesis.

The teachings in Chartres were kept totally free from any professional training—therefore the term *Liberal* Arts. Professional education, in so far as it existed at the time, was given elsewhere. These professional disciplines (such as law and medicine) were called 'dirty', because they could be used to earn money. At Chartres, only the 'generally' human was taught, which means that it was really a Spiritual Schooling Path, an echo of the old mysteries.

Today's adult education, on the other hand, is very much characterized by professional training. The various faculties of universities generally offer professional training courses *par excellence*. The overall aim of this book, however, is to 'humanize' professional education again, to make it socially fruitful again and allow it to become a Schooling Path. Thus, the main objective of Chartres becomes once more the innermost aim of a modern professional adult education.

In an esoteric book, *The Chymical Wedding of Christian Rosenkreutz* by Johann Valentin Andreae, published in 1616, the transition from the old Schooling Path to the new is described. It is expressed in imaginative incidents that speak for themselves and may be significant for our subject. The Seven Liberal Arts are described as seven kings that are beheaded, but whose blood is caught and kept, each in a separate vase. The main person of the seven day story, Christian Rosenkreutz, witnesses all the events. He also sees (by accident?) how the bodies of the seven kings are put on to boats and rowed out to sea. There, he sees a flame floating above each of the boats. These are the spirits of the beheaded kings. He knows now that these pictures represent the transformation of his own forces of knowledge. The transformation of his soul has led him on to the new path to the spirit.

These pictures will not be interpreted further here, especially as the story is much longer than just indicated. We may, however, ask ourselves whether some aspects of these images re-emerge when the Seven Life Processes are changed into the Seven Learning Processes by the activity of the ego.

The old life is beheaded because human beings have become head people, learning to observe accurately with their senses. However, the activation of the life processes also re-enlivens the twelve senses, and we learn to see the essential through the senses.

By activating the Seven Life Processes we can also transform them into a soul quality. This leads to new inner faculties in thinking, feeling and will. In this process, the first three and the last four steps form a unity manifesting as a kind of '*Trivium*' and '*Quadrivium*.'

It is not far-fetched, therefore, to regard the transformation of the originally body-bound life processes into learning processes that are oriented towards the senses (as well as ensouling them in thinking, feeling and will), as a rebirth of the Seven Liberal Arts. For this purpose, the actively learning ego has to become a flame. It has to burn what it has taken in from outside so that the new in us may be born individually. In the adult way of learning, the ego has to become a flame, and thereby it is able to awaken the slumbering will that is working in our organism.

Making this possible may become a fundamental principle of adult education.

Part Two:
Forms of Learning

7. The Relationship between Adult Educator and Adult Participant

When we try to determine the relationship between adult educator and participant in adult education, we notice immediately that this relationship is strongly shaped by the past. This is even reflected in the terminology: lecturer—student, teacher—trainee, master—apprentice. This hierarchy of names is suggestive. As we have been trying to describe this relationship of two adults as a type of encounter (see Chapter 4), let us speak in what follows of the *adult educator* and the *participant*. These are terms that denote, as much as possible, a relationship based on equality.

In ancient cultures we find repeatedly that those who taught were the learned ones, the advanced ones, those who knew. They were the gurus, the initiates, who revealed their wisdom through a prescribed, strictly regulated, learning path. The apprentice/pupil would look up to them with reverence, full of devotion and faithful to what was being taught.

An after-effect of these two basic attitudes can still be felt in our present-day educational institutions and universities. Overcoming these attitudes requires an arduous effort on the parts of both adult educator and participant. This is shown clearly in the two varieties of: 'compulsive striving' for authority and 'destructive rebellion' against it.

It is often no easy task to help the participants take on full responsibility for their own learning process. For the adult educators, too, it is difficult to apply and shape their greater experience, their knowledge and skills in a particular area in such a way as to support the participants on their path, without coercion.

Firstly, however, this requires a change of attitude and behaviour by adult educators. Their experience, their skill and knowledge are to be nothing but the means to further the development of others. Instead of being a leader, the adult educator of today should be an 'enabler', who experiences gratefulness and joy because he is allowed to contribute to the development of a companion human being. Being further advanced in a certain area implies the task of 'making something possible' for another person—making it possible for them to learn, showing a possible way.

Secondly, what about the participants, the students, the pupils, the apprentices? How, in the process of 'Learning how to Learn', can they develop and recognize the attitude that will show them that Adult Learning requires an independent, self-igniting ego activity and ego warmth? That Adult Learning always requires independent judgement, the attitude of somebody who is asking questions, seeking, investigating, and researching? Any kind of passive, dependent accepting that is based on faith in authority must disappear. Only then can the participant make it possible for the adult educator truly to become a servant of the Adult Learning Process. The two new attitudes support and determine each other. They make each other possible.

A useful thought for the participants is the following:

— Never *accept* anything totally before it has been fully understood.

— Never simply *reject* anything before it has been fully understood.

What is useful for adult educators is to look at how they deal with questions. There are two main categories of questions: Questions that are directed towards content and which seemingly require a thought for an answer, such as: What is it? Why? What for? Then there are those questions that have an intentional character demanding a decision, which seem to ask for instruction, such as: How should I do it? What am I to do? What am I to become? What is my next step?

The adult educator may very easily be tempted to answer the first type of question in terms of *content*. Then he might bring the second type of question to a conclusion by making a decision and then *giving instructions*. By doing so the adult educator would again relapse into the old authority role, thus impairing the independent learning process.

The reverse process may often trigger off a different kind of learning:

— With questions regarding content, we could show the participants a *path* that would enable them to find their own answer.
— With questions regarding the will—which are often existential in nature—we should give the participants a leading *image* that will enable them to find their own independent direction.

In other words:

— To show a *path for the will* in answer to *thought* questions;
— To answer *will* questions with a *thought picture* that leaves the will of the other person free.

Once, when asked: 'How can I understand the power behind life?' Rudolf Steiner answered: 'Study rhythm.' Then, when young people in the early twenties of this century asked him what they could do about the crucial events of the century, he said that they should build a chariot for Michael, the Spirit of our Times. Since he had already said a good deal about the Spirit of the Times, this picture had an awakening effect on the will.

If participant and adult educator are to shape the learning process together, it is essential for them to foster their mutual relationship, for this human relationship becomes the vehicle that is to carry the learning process. It was already mentioned in Chapter 2 that, during their schooling as adult educators, they must learn to have 'helping conversations'. The participants, on the other hand, must develop the ability while 'Learning how to Learn' to relate to the adult educators in such a way that the latter can give of their best potential. Learning how to respond and relate to their teacher can be very beneficial for the participants in their learning process.

In practice, there are always tensions, blockages, conflicts between adult educators and participants. The most wonderful results for the Schooling Path of both can occur whenever both groups succeed in regarding these as an essential ingredient of the learning process and deal with them in a constructive, human way. This, then, brings us to the third level of the relationship between participant and adult educator.

First level—Conscious aim and *meaning of the relationship* shape the learning process.

*Second level—*It is necessary constantly to foster the *human encounter.* This may lead to some Destiny Learning.

*Third level—*In the sense of the three paths of learning (see Chapter 3), the learning process also includes the *Spiritual Schooling Path.*

The relationship between adult educator and participant manifests a new dimension. The adult educator becomes an advisory friend, concerning the problems that the participants encounter when they cross over the threshold between the sense world and the spiritual world.

Since even in intensive professional training courses people today are more and more confronted with threshold experiences, this is not as remote as people often tend to think. Wherever this third level becomes effective, it will intensify the other two.

In summary, it can be said that a threefold relationship is to be striven for:

1. Making the learning process possible and shaping it cooperatively;
2. Human encounter, including learning through destiny;
3. Advisory friendship, where the understanding of the indications given will become the essential aspect of the schooling and research path.

At the first level, the adult educators are far ahead of the participants in teaching content, technical knowledge and experience, otherwise they should not be adult educators. This means that they are experts in a technical sense. They make their knowledge, their skills and their experience available to the participants.

At the second level, which refers to the human relationship, the aim will always be to foster mutuality. This is the only way to nurture a true relationship. The weaknesses and strengths, the idiosyncrasies, the possibilities and impossibilities of both are considered.

At the third level, however, it becomes obvious that, here, the participants are the focus of attention and that adult educators have to subordinate themselves to the unique Schooling Path of the other. They have to relate to the participants in a serving way. In that sense the first and the third level are polar opposites, while the second level creates a middle balance.

To move around these three attitudes and modes of behaviour in a meaningful way is the task of the adult educator as well as of the participant. It is a part of the 'Learning how to Learn' of every adult, and of the professional path of the adult educator continuously to strive for these aims. Wherever this threefold mode of behaviour is already being practised, it is often discussed also on a regular basis between the adult educators and the participants (and thereby improved), so that the learning process comes to an optimal unfolding of its inherent possibilities.

8. Course Design—The Integrated Programme

Courses often have a pioneer-like beginning, followed by a period of growth and maturity, and then a gradual fading away. That is to say, a birth phase, a life phase, and a process of dying; in other words, a biography. There are those courses as well that take place once and then, as it were, die immediately. It is not unusual either for a new course to be run three times before it is successful and accepted. The second time a course is run, crises are not uncommon. The third time, finally, it has left its infancy behind. In the process of a course, a great number of things happen between, through and with the participants. At the end of the course it has become an 'event' that lives on in the participants and adult educators. In short, a course is a *being* that is given life by the participants and the adult educators together.

It may either be a fragmentary being, even one that makes people ill, or else an organic, integral, awakening, developing being, that has a healing effect on participant and adult educator, awakening their will as well.

Naturally, almost everything depends on the way the course is structured and run. Therefore, there is an increasing tendency to shape a course as an organism in which all parts complement, support, deepen and mutually determine each other. This is then called an Integrated Programme. The life of the course is determined by the way and the intensity of the preparatory work. (See also Chapter 4).

8.1. The Integrated Programme

An Integrated Programme may be shaped from different points of view. In the following, a few integration features shall be described which are often in opposition. This is why it is very important to choose an integration feature according to the nature and aim of the course. For instance, an art education requires a different kind of integration from that of a scientific education or a technical education. A well-known and very general integration feature is the integration of the learning elements themselves.

8.1.1. Integration of the Elements of Learning
The following learning elements may be distinguished:

Lectures/talks; *Group Work*; *Artistic Activities*; *Specific Exercises*; *Project Work*; *Beginning and End of the Day*.

Each of the elements requires a different attitude by the adult educator and the participant that stimulates different faculties and highlights a different aspect of the learning process. Each learning element is different in nature. In the lecture, the subject matter is assimilated in a listening way. In group work, it is worked through together. Artistic activities are of a creative, experiential, discovering nature. Exercises train a certain ability. Project work demands, among other things, the application of what we have learned, requires self-discipline and responsibility, appeals to a realistic way of planning our time and many other things. Therefore each of these learning elements speaks to different parts of our being.

In practice, these learning elements are often combined, such as in the teaching conversation, in learning groups, artistic exercises, etc. The point, however, is to shape these basic learning processes into one whole, namely in such a way that the elements mutually reinforce each other, complement each other in a deeper sense, so that an organism of learning elements may come about. Indeed, it is often surprising how many different ways there are in which the participants experience what is essential, make personal discoveries, break through to sudden insights. With one person this happens during a lecture, with another through an incident in a group conversation, and with a third through an experience with colour, sound or form. The essential thing, however, is that this breakthrough may happen because of the organic configuration of the learning elements.

8.1.2. Vertical and Horizontal Integration

— *Vertical integration* has to do with the order of the programme on a given day;
— *Horizontal integration* refers to structure of the programme over days, weeks, months and even years.

Vertical integration produces a direct connection of all learning elements in one day. If, for instance, at the beginning of the day, an important question is presented, it will then be discussed in the groups, deepened in the next lecture, experienced by means of exercises in the afternoon, and dealt with artistically at the end of the day. On looking back over the day, the participant needs to discover what was essential. This can be done in many different ways, but the main objective is to integrate the day into one organic whole. Vertical integration is a very important aspect of adult education, since the day rhythm stimulates the ego rhythm.

The ego lives during the 24 hours of day and night. Whenever the day learning process is fully integrated, the assimilation that takes place during the night and in dream consciousness is intensified as well. This often leads to an increased awareness for learning, a stronger motivation and a reinforced will to learn, because the vertical integration strongly stimulates the ego consciousness.

The essential feature of horizontal integration is repetition. It is common knowledge that little can be achieved without regular practice over days and weeks. Developing a new ability, or faculty, establishing real understanding, becoming familiar with something new, takes time. In this respect the rhythm and the structure of the sessions are decisive.

In practice, these two directions of integration are often in conflict with each other. The daily integration interferes with the horizontal integration. The horizontal may appear to be an alien element in a day. The question is how to integrate the two directions, since both are so valuable. One possibility, for instance, would be to have a daily thematic structure (vertical), introducing another aspect each day (horizontal) so that the week in its totality would be integrated around one subject. This weekly structure has to be shaped in a rhythmic way by means of exercises, group work, artistic activities, etc. (horizontal). All of these will, of course, support the topic of the respective day.

A good way of integrating vertical and horizontal is to start the day with an exercise that is bridge-building. For instance, in the morning the thread of the previous evening is taken up, thus building a bridge to the present session. In some courses, the participants themselves are asked to prepare and present this bridging activity. Then, at the end of the day, the whole day is reviewed and the next day prepared. This, too, is bridge-building by nature. Adult educators who believe that they have no time for this way of beginning and reviewing a day, underestimate, in learning terms, the productivity of these processes and the immensity of the loss resulting from this neglect.

Each time the horizontal and vertical are successfully linked in an integrative way, the learning process is considerably reinforced. However, although the ideas above have proved to be excellent, it is obvious that this kind of Integrated Programme can really be carried out only by a team of adult educators that is integrated. Everything depends on their real co-operation. In Chapter 15 we will come back to this.

8.1.3. Integration of Content

Here, the focus is on a particular question or a formulated subject towards which all the activities are directed. The author still remembers, with much pleasure, a one-week course that focused on the question of 'What is colour?' All activities were dedicated to this subject: light experiments, nature observations, colour eurythmy, painting, verses and even lectures—all of them deepening this one question. At the end of the week it was not a *subject* any more but had become a colour *experience* with many new and unexpected questions that continued to have an effect for a long time.

It is important to choose one subject that can be clearly defined and is then worked through over a longer time, from many points of view, and by various means. Most programmes are too full of content. This may lead to superficiality and an abstract way of dealing with the subject.

One variant on *content* integration is *aim* integration. A specific aim is to be achieved with a particular group of participants, for instance: to experience group development, or to recognize laws of growth. However, this is verging on being part of a research process.

8.1.4. Integration of Rhythm

Far too little research has been done on the question of how to include rhythms into the course structure and how to give a rhythmic element to all activities. What is certain, however, is that making a structure rhythmical has an integrative effect. This would become obvious, in an opposite way, if suddenly the starting times were changed, one-sided activities were overemphasized, parts of the programme were unexpectedly exchanged, etc.

After all, the human being is a rhythmical being and therefore should be given the opportunity to take part in shaping a rhythmical, living course. Each individual learning element has to be shaped in a rhythmic way. It is interesting to observe our breathing while listening to a lecture: difficulty in breathing with interminable speakers, exhaustion when listening to people who use many words to say very little.

In general, it can be said that non-rhythmical processes have a damaging effect, while a rhythmical course structure may be healing and health bestowing. Important rhythms are for instance: daily rhythm, three-day rhythm, weekly rhythm, monthly and yearly rhythm. The point here is to accompany the ego, through the particular way of teaching, in its processes of incarnation and excarnation.

a) Daily rhythm: As already mentioned above, this rhythm has to do with ego development (vertical integration). In general, people feel different in the morning, at midday or in the evening. This is why often an attempt is made to organize the learning elements accordingly. However, experience has shown that it is not so much a question of the learning elements as such, but rather of the way they are dealt with. Eurythmy after lunch can be both agreeable and very disturbing; a lecture before supper can be exhausting or reviving.

b) Three-day rhythm: A three-day course has a completely different effect from a course of two or four days. Here, the relationship of the ego to time is important.

1st day: Building up of the course: understanding the past.
2nd day: Experiencing the present.
3rd day: Preparing the future. This rhythm is very effective for short courses.

c) Weekly rhythm: The weekly rhythm has to do with soul development. It is the developmental rhythm *par excellence*. Historically, the week as an idea emerged around 3000 BC, when humanity's consciousness started to turn more inward. Each day of the week has a character of its own, together they form a unity. Courses structured in terms of weeks, with each week having a subject or goal of its own, have proved to be very worthwhile in adult education, since, after all, soul development and learning process are closely related. The fact that the course never lasts a full week is of little importance since the Sunday is regarded as a rest-day.

d) Monthly rhythm: This has to do with our habits. It seems to take us four weeks to acquire a new skill, habit or quality. Thought models and methods also seem to take four weeks to 'settle down' in our 'body of habit'. The monthly integration may even be strengthened if the structure consists of four one week sessions, with the four weeks forming one whole. Weekly rhythm and monthly rhythm reinforce each other. The same goes for a structure of three one week sessions, with the fourth week for integration.

e) Yearly rhythm: The yearly rhythm has to do with our physical body. We count our age in years. Many adult educators demand a yearly structure because only then has the subject matter penetrated the whole human being. Thereby we have made it our own and can apply it independently in the outside world. It is good, for instance, to work on a specific subject for a year, investigating it and living with it, before giving public lectures on it. This rhythm would then have an agreeable effect on many of the listeners.

Much more, of course, could be mentioned about the rhythmical structuring of the learning processes. Here, however, this aspect is mentioned only because it is a means of integrating the programme.

8.1.5. Project Integration

One form of learning that is now being generally recognized, is 'project-learning'. Here, a certain task is given which allows us to put everything we have learned into practice. To do so, we must find the appropriate form of application.

In this context, it is of great importance to overcome the will barrier. One of the simplest ways is to present the result of our learning efforts, in an artistic form, to the other participants at the end of the course. This in itself has a considerable integrative effect.

Projects may be done individually or in groups. In the latter case, the co-operation of the participants is an essential component. This is why an experienced project facilitator is needed. Project-learning takes many different forms and is gaining more and more importance. There are short courses that are structured around projects, with theory, methods and exercises being included as required.

8.1.6. Integration of Structure

It can be experienced that, when people listen to lectures, the *content* of the lecture often appeals to a critical element and even antipathies. *Personal* aspects and examples that are given in the lecture, however, have a connecting effect. It is the basic *structure* of a lecture that affects the will. Therefore, a clear and archetypal basic structure may help the participants to awaken their will, especially in longer courses. However, the opposite may well happen as well. An incoherent, arbitrarily structured course makes the participants uncertain and has a paralysing effect. A course, on the other hand, which is over structured, too rigid and planned in too much detail has a similar effect. That is to say, it demotivates the participants.

In the following a few basic course structures are given:

— A *twelve-week semester* was divided into three times four weeks, with each week being given a learning objective of its own. The general objective was the development of social skills. The first four weeks: learning about social questions, concepts, impulses. The second four weeks: dealing with the same questions about 'human relationships' and experiencing them. The third four weeks: practising. In the second and third semesters, these three objectives were then deepened and further worked through. The structure of the four weeks was three plus one. That is to say: three weeks of intensive taking-in and learning, where the elements mainly worked with were concepts, experiencing and practising. The fourth week was fully dedicated to digesting, deepening and integrating the first three weeks.

No new subject matter was then introduced. This basic structure was discussed every week and put up on the wall to give an overall picture. Consequently, the participants always knew where they were in the learning process, and why and how everything was connected with the whole. Variations of the basic structure could be included during the process as required. The participants were strongly involved in carrying responsibility. The repetitive rhythm of the basic structure 3 + 1, 3 + 1, 3 + 1 had a motivating effect.

— Quite a different structure is the so-called *staircase structure*. Every week, in a nine-week course, the focus was on one main subject or question. The nine subjects, however, built on each other. Each week the foundation for the following week was being built, going one step ahead, so that the impression was had of climbing a ladder. Since the thread running through this course was the Spiritual Schooling Path, this seemed to be the appropriate structure.

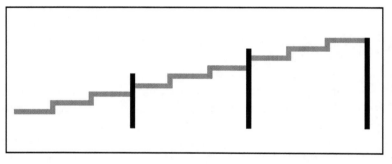

Diagram 6

— There are also structures that *mirror around a middle*. In terms of weeks, this gives the picture as shown in Diagram 7. The first week's work reappears in the ninth week in a changed form. The second and the eighth week are likewise mirror pictures, etc.

The weeks themselves are organically coherent, with the fifth week as the central element giving meaning to the other weeks. This requires a team of adult educators who work well together, and who have to prepare meticulously. This format may also be used for three, five or seven days or several weeks.

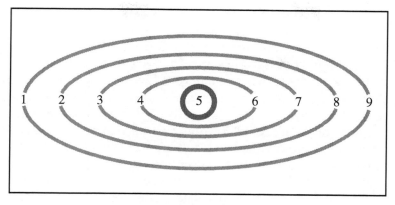

Diagram 7

— Moreover there are *two-week structures*: one week of taking in, with applying and deepening in the second week.

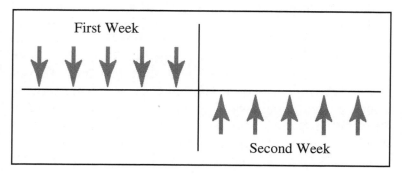

Diagram 8

— Basic formats in *three parts* are quite frequent as well. For instance, under the heading: Past, Present, Future. Or: Understanding, Experiencing, Implementing.

Besides the above mentioned formats—'3 + 1 format', staircase format, mirror format, and three- or fourfold format—there are many others. The main thing is that the format is based on a developmental process that is in harmony with the human being.

8.1.7. Integration of the Learning Process Itself

There has already been some experience in structuring a course in full accordance with the Sevenfold Learning Process. In short courses, it has proved very worthwhile, but only if the participants are familiar with the Sevenfold Learning Process. (See Chapter 5.) Successively, all activities are structured around the respective processes (observing, relating, digesting, etc.). In doing so particular emphasis is placed on the individualizing of Step 4. In this form of integration, particular didactic attention must be given to the transitions. In the author's view, this sevenfold process is one of the most important approaches to an organic, integrative way of designing and conducting courses. It is something that points to a future way of working.

It must be mentioned here that artistic activities, too, may have an integrative and strengthening effect on the learning process. Art may very well deepen the learning process. The prerequisite, however, is that the artistic activity should hold back all other objectives, serving exclusively the learning process of the participant. This is why it might be better to speak of an 'artistic learning activity'. There has been very promising experience with this at the *Alanus-Kunsthochschule* in Alfter, Germany. Thus, artistic activity, when used in the right way, becomes an important catalyst of the Adult Learning Process. If, one day, the universities should discover and apply this possibility, their courses could certainly be shortened and intensified as well.

8.2. The Staff Group

When the course is being planned and implemented, as well as with any attempt at restructuring and improving courses, co-operation within the staff group is of essential importance. During the course, 'stock taking' and conversations should take place regularly. The working together of the staff group, before and during the course, has an integrating effect. This, however, takes time and needs creativity. Since many adult educators have never learned to work together creatively with—often very different—colleagues, this is the 'bottleneck' of an integrated way of designing and conducting courses. Chapter 16 will go into this in more detail.

9. Learning Activities

In many educational institutions it became obvious that reviewing the learning processes contributed considerably to deepening the way people learn. Taking in content or having experiences does not yet constitute conscious learning. Only reviewing and evaluating these experiences was found to lead to conscious learning.

There is a great variety of methods on how to conduct reviews. The following will try to bring some order into the objectives and methods. To begin with, let us distinguish three main methods: the *review*, the *evaluation*, and the *preview*.

The following is based on the assumption that these three methods are to serve the learning process of the participants and not only the needs of the staff.

9.1. The Review

The review is based on people's ability to become observers of their own being and functioning, to remember the past and to see these images in front of their mind's eye. In doing so, time is imagined as pictures in space. They gain an overview, the pictures speak for themselves. Any personal judgement is held back as much as possible.

It is amazing what can be seen when looking back over the day in the evening. This activity makes us become aware of the actual learning process. Experiences are looked at from a higher perspective, thus revealing their meaning and their inner connections. It is a way of 'spiritualizing' the learning process.

A review may be done for a particular day, a week, a whole course, a project, etc.

Biography courses or workshops, for instance, are based on reviewing our lives. Reviewing, however, has to be learned. It is a faculty that could be taught by the adult educator. This can be done in many ways. For instance:

— The adult educator may remind the participants of the main points and ask them to contribute the details;
— The participants may be asked to keep a diary in which they record what is essential to them. Later the participants may share this with each other;
— The levels, phases and processes may be linked together and represented graphically;
— The course, or part of it, may be represented in the form of a poem, a painting, a scene or a sculpture.

The teaching methods of the staff will, of course, be influenced by the faculties of the participants. Often we discover with a shock how much is lost in Adult Learning if no review is made. In that case, a great deal sinks down that is undigested. This leads to mental or emotional 'indigestion'. A genuine chance to learn is missed if the review is omitted. To review means in a certain sense 'to harvest'. It is a process that requires some ego-activity. We create a distance from ourselves and look on our own past like an objective spectator.

At school and university many people have learned to criticize immediately what they take in, rather than to look at their experiences in a pictorial way. This means that first they have to 'unlearn' to get rid of old habits.

9.2. The Evaluation

The next step is the evaluation that is based on the objective review, but takes it a step further. It is based on the individual's ability to evaluate learning processes, thereby establishing their relative importance. The evaluation is very individual, for, what is an important discovery to one person, the other person has long since known. In other words, the point is to find out what is the most valuable for our own path of learning. This always involves self-knowledge to a certain extent. In the process of evaluation unpleasant, frustrating learning experiences often yield the highest results, if we are able objectively to discover their 'value'.

What has to be added to the outer learning process, is our inner behaviour. The outer and the inner are looked at together here. Joyful and embarrassing elements play a part. We become aware of deeply hidden motives and forces. The learning process is examined with the 'whole' human being in mind, not just the learning process and content. In doing so we often discover how we learn, and where and what the barriers are. This may help us to find a way to overcome the three learning barriers. (See Chapter 2.)

It is obvious that accompanying this kind of process makes high demands on the didactic skill of the adult educator. As soon as the evaluation degenerates into a value judgement of emotions, stuck opinions and judgements, it ceases to be a learning process and may even have a damaging effect. This is why purposeful, structured evaluation methods are often used that provide specific questions and definite objective criteria.

Regarding the learning of social skills, it has become obvious in group work, for instance, that evaluation of a group process is one of the most important means of learning. Even more than when doing the review, we may become aware of how many extremely important learning moments there are every day, the actual value of which shows itself only during a good evaluation.

Another possible method to use is an artistic activity such as painting or modelling. The participants try to express in colours and forms what has happened. This helps us to become aware of what is essential. Well-led conversations, too, are an opportunity to discover and become aware of a great deal. Prepared questionnaires are a possible aid as well, although we must realize that they might cover up important specific events that are not mentioned in the questionnaire.

Likewise, keeping a diary may be very fruitful. In a few words we can record, for instance:

a) What have I learned today?
b) How have I learned it?
c) What new questions, decisions and discoveries as well as conclusions result from it?

9.3. The Preview

Previews have the objective of preparing the future. This requires a different attitude from that of the review. To review means: to *look at* the past; to *evaluate* means: to *experience, judge* and *investigate* the past; to *plan* means: *to scan* the future with our will. It is part of a planning process to look at questions such as: What is the next feasible step? What plans shall we make? How can we improve things? It is based on the two above-mentioned activities. Often, courses or learning processes are judged and condemned without doing a proper review and evaluation first. This may lead to very disturbing misjudgements, both among the participants and the people running the course.

In other words, the preview emerges in a natural way out of the review and evaluation. Here, even more than with the other two activities, the staff must allow the preview to arise completely out of the group of participants. Our will knows the future already, but the essential thing is to allow this will to arise in consciousness.

Adult education is an awakening of the will. Therefore, these three activities may make a considerable contribution to this awakening, if practised regularly in their natural order.

9.4. Implications Regarding Life After Death

When considering learning as an integration of three paths of learning, as described in Chapter 3, and trying to investigate the spiritual background of the three above-mentioned learning activities, it becomes obvious that a similar process takes place in the case of Destiny Learning. The range of this extends, of course, over several lives on earth.

After completing their lives on earth, people also find themselves confronted with a process of evaluation that also takes place in three steps, analogous to the learning activities described above. Further details on this may be found in the numerous publications of spiritual science, so it will be mentioned just briefly here.

In the first three days after death a review of our life takes place. The life-forces are withdrawing from the physical body. The deceased see their whole life unfolding around them in a kind of panorama. Whatever they experienced in the time between birth and death becomes visible in powerful pictures in the space around them. This already gives a totally different meaning to their lives from the memories they used to have. Many of those people who have had near-death experiences can testify to this panoramic review.

The second stage, lasting about one third of our last life on earth, is very different. It is a kind of self-evaluation. We go through everything others have experienced that was caused by the way we behaved, the deeds we committed. Moreover, we have to give up everything that still binds the soul to the body, and much more. This process, called 'Kamaloka' in the relevant literature, is at the same time an evaluation—everything we have done and experienced in life, the positive aspects as well as the negative ones, is evaluated. Steadily, this determines the will to make up for mistakes, improve shortcomings, find the task for our next life, in order then to pre-shape our future Destiny Learning. This is a kind of preview. This means that learning on earth, in its three forms of *review*, *evaluation*, *preview,* is the reflection of a process that always take place after death under the guidance of the powers of destiny. The way the divine beings develop us, is practised in advance in the Adult Learning Process by means of *review*, *evaluation*, *preview*. Doing so, we practise a truly divine way of learning, thereby also connecting the three paths of learning. (See Chapter 3.) In 'Learning to Learn', every adult should acquire the faculties necessary to review, evaluate and preview.

These archetypal pictures of life after death can teach adult educators how to handle these learning processes. So far only these three have been described as specific, deepening activities or categories. Becoming more specific would give rise to other learning objectives.

9.5. More on Evaluation

The *Evaluation* may also be used in connection with the following:

Learning of conceptual material. Then it refers to the digestion of content, the understanding, the overview of the content, the open questions, the thought processes and methods that take place, etc. The actual process of cognitive learning can be intensified in this way.

Evaluating the Learning Process. This relates to the questions: 'What have I learned?', 'How did this learning take place at an outer and an inner level?', 'What new questions arise in me as a result?' It is also very helpful here to use the Seven Steps of the Learning Process. (See Chapter 5.) 'Learning how to Learn' is intensified thereby.

The Evaluation of How the Group of Participants is Functioning. As much as possible the group should be made to share responsibility in the programme. This increases their sense of being co-responsible for the course. Regular evaluation of their group processes in this respect enhances their responsibility and participation

The Integration of the Elements of Learning. Many courses have very different forms of learning: lectures, group work, art lessons, exercises, etc. The three learning activities are very helpful when integrating these forms of learning into one organic whole. The horizontal and the vertical formats are evaluated, the coherence deepened, the parts brought together, etc. (See Chapter 8.)

The Process of Development. Here, the development of the individual participant is to be distinguished from the development of the group. As every adult educator knows, the group itself also goes through different phases and crises of development. Review, evaluation and preview are very supportive activities to accompany their crises. Crises that are worked through often provide the most valuable learning opportunities for the participants. The individual processes of development may be guided both in small groups and in individual conversations.

There are *many further specific aims* the evaluation can refer to. The advantage of specific aims is that they may be clearly defined, thus allowing them to penetrate more deeply. Their disadvantage is that they often prevent the destiny element in the learning process from coming to the surface, which consequently then becomes lost.

A practical guide to group evaluation can be found in Chapter 10.

10. How to Design and Use Exercises

Using specific exercises in adult education is increasing in importance. Their design, their objectives, their didactic application and evaluation, are issues about which many adult educators are concerned. This is why they are dealt with in a separate chapter. Using exercises takes place in three different phases, each of which has its own character.

10.1. Preparation

First, the learning objective has to be clearly established, for there is a range:

Category I: There are, for instance, many little exercises that serve the purpose of 'becoming aware of something'; they awaken people's consciousness, are 'eye openers' by nature, but this does not mean that they develop any particular skill.

Category II: This is the learning objective to acquire a *specific skill*. This may include anything from learning to embroider, to learning to drive or read balance sheets. This takes more time and repetition before it begins to emerge as a skill.

Category III: This is the learning objective of developing a *new ability,* or *faculty.*

By way of repeating some sentences we have heard, we may, for instance, discover much about what promotes and what impedes listening (Category I). In other words: a *discovering* learning objective. A totally different exercise promotes proper listening (Category II) until the *ability* of concentrated listening has developed. A third exercise demanding quite different forces will lead only very gradually to the *ability* to become aware of the thoughts, feelings and will impulses stirring behind the spoken word (Category

III). An exercise of this nature is for instance the so-called *three-level exercise* that needs to be practised over a longer period before it becomes a genuine ability. This is a perception exercise where people listen to a story of a real life incident being told by one of their number and sequentially try:

1) To perceive the narrator's process of *thinking* behind the sentences (the *composition* of the story, and *how* the thoughts are being linked);
2) To sense the varied *feelings* accompanying the story that is being told;
3) Finally, intuitively to sense the *will intention* that is expressed while the story is being told (Why did they choose *this* story? What *effect* do they want it to have? What is the *motive* in telling it?).

The numerous artistic exercises, which often serve the purpose of sensitizing the senses, have a learning objective of their own. This is not to say, however, that many artistic activities or exercises may not serve certain aims of promoting the learning process and/or therapeutic, hygienic or educational aspects.

One last Category (IV) may be oriented towards specific research aims almost amounting to exploring, investigating. Biologists might do modelling exercises to get a better understanding of the metamorphosis of plants; certain exercises involving the regular observation of the weather may serve nature research, etc.

Even if further learning objectives may be found, one thing is certain: namely that in adult education we must have clear learning objectives in mind, since otherwise practising becomes an unintelligible game that cannot be evaluated afterwards.

So, the First Step is to establish the learning objective. The Second Step—designing the appropriate exercises—is usually a trial and error process. It is very desirable to try out the exercise with some colleagues, improving it until it 'fits' and we are reasonably familiar with it. This provides us with a first temporary form that may then be improved regularly.

Important criteria for this design are:

— The exercise needs to motivate the participants in a meaningful way (the Fourth Learning Process: Individualizing), and to contain a precise procedure and a timetable;

— The exercise, or a configuration of exercises, should have the potential of developing into a faculty, if this is laid down in the learning objective (the Sixth Learning Process: Growing Faculties);

— In this context, it is extremely important that the exercise should be based on a kind of archetype, such as the threefold or fourfold image of the human being.

— We should be clear about what kind and what number of participants the exercise is designed for. Already when preparing it, a number of review and evaluation questions should be formulated.

— The exercises should be kept as simple as possible. Experience has shown that not every exercise can be used by every adult educator. Therefore it is necessary for the adult educators to check the exercises they are intending to use. This has to do with the fact that it is decisive how the exercise is carried through with the participants. Here, the skills, experience and knowledge, the strengths and weaknesses of the adult educators play an important part.

10.2. Implementation

Here, everything depends on the 'how'. A good exercise may be done in a boring way, a bad one may still become a decisive learning event. This depends, among other things, on the adult educators' presence of mind and their ability to deepen and make conscious what is happening by means of purposeful and well-directed interventions. The exercise itself remains a framework making something possible. The following elements ought to be considered:

- To do an exercise, a special situation is needed in which something may happen. Therefore the physical environment has to be prepared accordingly, and a suitable mood for the exercise has to be created.
- The exercise needs to be explained: the procedure, its meaning and the learning objective. With successful exercises, these aspects are often left out after some time because they seem so obvious that it is assumed to be clear to everybody. Thereby, however, we omit to stimulate the participants' independent judgement.
- Adult educators should be very careful with their words. Typically, much too much is said, in too confusing and too unclear a way. It is helpful to write important sentences down beforehand. Many exercises are spoilt because adult educators talk too much and keep repeating themselves. An exercise is something that needs to be done. Having to listen unnecessarily is distracting and demotivating.
- The rhythmic repetition of exercises is an essential element, for this alone allows it to develop into a skill, and ultimately into a faculty. It is amazing what richness a simple observation exercise may have if the same one is repeated every day. The effort we have made during the day is assimilated at night bringing new possibilities the following day.
- The relationship between adult educator and participant has to be cared for continuously, since the way the two relate engenders the life-stream of the exercise. The relationship should be an investigating, researching one, that encourages and stimulates.
- The whole process should have a building rather than a fixing effect. For this purpose the adult educators may make use of their experiences with the so-called Subsidiary Exercises as a source of inspiration. (See Chapter 5.)
- The basic attitude should be joyful, warm and human, leave the participant free, and have an artistic style.

10.3. Evaluation

The experiences caused by these kinds of exercises will complete the learning process only if followed by a purposeful review and evaluation. Further details about evaluation as a learning activity may be found in Chapter 9. The evaluation must be aimed at the given learning objective. When using exercises, the evaluation is an essential part of the learning process. A bad, arbitrary, superficial evaluation will impair the value of exercising.

It is best when the evaluation takes place immediately after the exercise, or at least on the same day. It can also be done from time to time while the exercise is being carried out. On the following day the experiences will already have changed considerably through the night, so that something different will result.

With the evaluation itself, the first thing to do is to gather the actual experiences. These are then evaluated with the help of questions such as:

a) What have I really learned from this?
b) How did it happen?
c) What are the new questions or thoughts arising in me as a consequence? In general, anything leading to an optimum way of learning is fruitful.

These short explanations will have shown that designing, implementing and evaluating exercises is a specific ability that should be learned and developed by the adult educator. It is an art in itself that requires adult educators to have been schooled for their profession. The most capable experts have sometimes failed because in their teaching they have never learned this art. One experience, however, is that many of the exercises that have been developed and tried out, will disappear again. Some, however, will remain, develop and prove viable. This is most likely because they have acquired an archetypal quality. The numerous exercises devised by

Rudolf Steiner for developing human faculties are of permanent value.

11. The Marriage of Art and Science in Adult Learning

It is important to distinguish between and understand the two areas of *artistic creativity* and *scientific research* as thoroughly as possible before trying to regard adult education as a higher synthesis of the two.

Let us look at art first. While engaged in an artistic activity people are in an exceptional state. Something is happening to the activity of their senses, their life processes and their soul forces. Many different kinds of connecting, reinforcing, unifying are taking place, in short: The twelve senses, the soul and the life-forces are being connected in many different ways. As Rudolf Steiner has explained, the senses are enlivened by the life processes, while the life processes are ensouled by artistic activity. During this process, certain reinforcements take place because there is a connection or rather an affinity between specific senses and specific life processes, for instance, between hearing and growth, colour vision and breathing, sensing temperature and warming, taste and the maintaining process, etc. In ancient phases of the evolution of humanity, these were still very much connected. They constituted something which, today, would be called clairvoyance. Even today they may still appear under pathological conditions, such as sleepwalking

The ensouling of the life processes leads to the symbioses of groups of life processes. Thus, the first three—*breathing, warming, nourishing*—lead to a new kind of thinking. The following four—*secreting (sorting)*, *maintaining*, *growing*, and *reproducing*—to a new kind of will. The rhythm between the two, to a new kind of feeling. The new thinking is active more in the way we enjoy art; the new will in the way we are artistically creative; the new feeling in the rhythmical alternation between observing art and practising art. This means that the artistic activity as such will develop new soul faculties. The aesthetically gifted person is characterized by ensouled life processes. Therefore, artistic activities may considerably strengthen and deepen the Sevenfold Learning Process. It is not far-fetched to say that adult education might take art for its bride, as a living component of all learning processes. The bride, however, needs a bridegroom. What, then, about science?

With scientific processes strict rules have to be followed; the word *disciplines* is used. The scientific path must be able to be described precisely, so that it becomes comprehensible to other people. It must always be possible to control scientific results and to communicate them to others. A systematic way of proceeding is a necessity; predictability is striven for; knowledge is the aim. Thus, the human as a cognizing being on one hand and as a creative, experiencing being on the other, are opposites.

It is neither possible nor necessary, here, to give a detailed description of the two paths, because we are mainly concerned with the question of the learning processes.

A first connection between the two may be found when realizing that artists cannot really understand what they have created, unless they subsequently investigate their artistic activity in a scientific way. The scientists, too, ought to realize that they cannot possibly embark on their scientific path without the previous intuitive notion that there is a mystery. This pre-scientific notion, however, is an artistic activity. In teaching, too, the cognitive process is always preceded by a question, and a subsequent evaluation is required to understand what has been done. In his excellent essay 'Art and Science as Related Concepts', Yehudi Menuhin has described this relationship as the artistic being female and the scientific being male. This is another indication that it is necessary and fruitful for the two to meet. Completeness only results when the two embark upon a marriage relationship. Art without knowledge and understanding degenerates into arbitrariness; science without art loses touch with life. In a healthy professional schooling, this marriage should be allowed to take place, not by putting the two side by side, but by a genuine integration. Here, art and science teachers who have been trained in a one-sided way are often a problem.

Someone who is truly seeking for knowledge strives to discover the idea, the essential, behind all forms of manifestation, and for this purpose has to step over the threshold between the world of phenomena and the spiritual world. True artists want to bring the living idea into manifestation in the sense-perceptible world. To do so they have to cross over the threshold from the spiritual to the sense-perceptible world. They make the invisible visible.

What do adult educators do? To understand what they want to teach, they must be scientists—to make it visible to others, however, they must be artists. It is a constant movement from the physical world to the idea, and from the spiritual world to the current learning situation. It is not enough for them to know and understand their subject; neither does it suffice that they are able to describe everything in an imaginative way. No, in every learning situation, adult educators must be able to celebrate within themselves the marriage of art and science. That is their Schooling Path. This makes it easier to understand why so many excellent artists are bad adult educators, and why so many outstanding scientists are practically unable to impart their knowledge and their skills to others.

In the marriage of these two basic attitudes a third element is required: The marriage needs to be blessed as well! Regarding adult educators, this means a moral element that is connected with renunciation, even a sacrifice, must be born. Their artistic achievement and their research effort may no longer have absolute priority; this has to be replaced by their striving to serve their companion human beings in their learning process. This is an essential, qualitative element that is not usually included in the profession of teacher. Where this willingness to serve does not exist, adult education should not be taken up as a profession. The three elements: *art*, *science* and *devoted service* to the development of other people, form a new threesome that represents a creative source for the adult educator.

If the learning process is then extended into the Spiritual Schooling Path, the marriage between artistic experience and scientific research becomes a necessity for the learning process itself. The aesthetic faculty of judgement, described in Chapter 14, comes closest to this. Our feeling life, then, is constantly breathing back and forth between experiencing feeling inwards and feeling, sensing judgement outwards. While the artists increase their world of feeling experiences, the scientists school their feelings to become discernment, discrimination and assessment in the world of thinking. It is at the threshold of the spiritual world, however, that one has to learn to experience this world. Without a researching attitude we are likely to lose our independent judgement and consequently may be overwhelmed by the powerful spiritual experiences. Without a heightened artistic sensing, we cannot experience this world at all. The crossing of the threshold itself—now seen as a learning process—has therefore two sides to it. We have to be able to cope with both if this crossing is to occur in a healthy way.

The adult educators who, due to their human moral qualities, have united both attitudes in themselves, can thereby support the learning process considerably. We must take into account that today most participants are likely to have threshold experiences. A supportive understanding is therefore urgently needed.

11.1. A New Art and a New Science?

Many educational institutions are wrestling with the question: How is it possible to find a new conception of art? What is even more uncertain is how it should be taught. The task of art has always been a cultural one. Its purpose has been to ennoble humanity, to be the foundation of our civilization. It was the great educator of the originally wild, untamed passions. What kind of people would we be without music, drama, painting, architecture, poetry, etc.? Incredible achievements have been made, and yet there is a simmering dissatisfaction concerning art. Something new has to come. A new aim? A new source?

The Mystery of Golgotha fundamentally changed our relationship to the earth. Just now, humanity is unconsciously crossing over the threshold of a supersensible world. This changes the nature of the soul as well as the relationship to the spiritual world.

Originally art was a form of revelation. It made the *supersensible* world visible in the *sense-perceptible* world. Should today's art not strive to become an art of resurrection, spiritualizing the earthly sense world?

From a revelational art to a resurrectional art: to follow this path, art has to unite with science and religion. Thus, art would become a religious path of knowing. A First Step would be to strive to tread the path from the sense world to the supersensible world and back to earth, with a religious attitude and faculties developed through practising art and science.

A Second Step would be to understand the appearance of the Christ in the etheric world as a leading image for our artistic work. This event shows itself as a death of consciousness in the etheric world, and a resurrection in the etheric world and in the human soul as well. The death in the consciousness of the Christ was caused by the materialism in *our* thinking, feeling and will; the resurrection by *his* deed of sacrifice changed this darkness into light.

If the new art, in keeping with our times, is to become a resurrectional art serving the earth and humanity, then the *Imitatio Christi (Imitation of Christ)* becomes the guide and the source of strength for the developmental path of the modern artist.

To spiritualize matter in this sense would be the task. Whoever looks at this kind of art may experience, given to them by this new art, the light shining in the darkness as a healing, helping process within themselves.

The great artists have always been initiates. It is also true today that anyone who wants to become an artist should also go the modern path of research while preparing for their vocation. The art will then show how far the artists have advanced on their spiritual path.

An important statement about this path of research may be found in Rudolf Steiner's Torquay lectures, elaborated by Bernard Lievegoed in *Schulungswege*.[8] In this book the individual Moon Path and the joint Saturn Path are described. It is stated that it will be necessary to follow this Saturn Path for some time before the new art can arise as a Sun Path between Moon Path and Saturn Path. The essential aspect of the Saturn Path is described as the involvement of the powers of destiny working between people. This is why the new art has to do with both the path of research and the powers of destiny. Here, too, an artistic education requires a synthesis of adult School Learning, Destiny Learning and the Path of Spiritual Research.

In an age in which our technology threatens to destroy nature, and humanity seems to be endangered by all kinds of inventions, it is justified to ask the questions: for *whom* is this new science and for *what* is it there? Just as the famous nuclear researcher Julius Oppenheimer stated, teaching pure science without basic moral considerations seems to have devastating effects. It should have been his duty, he said, to teach his highly gifted students the morality that has to accompany such talents! Applied science, that is, technology, also needs to be humanized. Here again, the adult educator is confronted with the task to teach in such a way that a *human* science may come about. Spiritual science shows a way in this direction. The didactic basis for a human way of teaching science consists, among other things, of continuously cultivating, and developing equally, the cognitive, as well as the aesthetic and moral judgement of the participants. In doing so we should strive to base the marriage of art and science on a morality serving the earth and humankind.

Within the framework of this book, it is not possible to elaborate on a new science. That it is needed, however, should be the conviction of every adult educator.

12. Our Biography as Destiny Learning in Adult Learning

In Chapter 3, the three paths of learning have been indicated. The second path of learning, 'Learning through Life or Destiny', described how we try to respond to the demands of our environment to the best of our faculties in the widest sense of the word; and that this confrontation with the world entails a learning process which often goes far beyond any School Learning. Studying human biographies will provide us with much information about this second path of learning, for the composition of a biography seems to be structured like a curriculum for a course of self-education. A full understanding of this second path of learning, the origin of it in former lives and the meaning of it for the future, is of paramount importance.

Whoever has to counsel many people who are in the second half of their lives, will soon discover that, for most of the clients, this path of learning through their destiny is partly blocked or at least problematic. We are often incapable of changing this or that pattern by ourselves. There is no more development, no new learning, we are stuck. What is amazing is that often, in these cases, destiny intervenes unexpectedly, almost forcing the person concerned to start moving again. In retrospect, an illness, a divorce, the loss of a job, an accident, an economic crisis, even a war, may prove to be highly significant for that person's biography. In this Chapter, however, regarding learning blockages, we will not look into the depths of biographical events, but merely focus on the Destiny Learning aspect of Adult Learning.

When observing life we can distinguish three areas that may later become a source of getting stuck:

1. Our education;
2. The organization we are working for;
3. Our profession.

These are the three areas, where we are formed or educated by our environment, that offer material for learning. They also become either the basis for further learning or lead to the kind of hardening that will later turn into a learning impediment. In the latter case we may speak of a deformation. Professional deformation has become a worrying phenomenon, for in our quickly changing environment many people are no longer able to keep up with the vast changes in their professional life.

12.1. Education

That the child learns in a way different from that of the adult has already been described repeatedly. From the human biography viewpoint, the transition from child school learning to Adult Learning should take place around the age of 21. From 21 onwards, our ego is fully available to monitor independent, active learning processes. With many people, however, too little of a change or no change at all takes place, and child school learning continues. It depends on the school education whether this change around the age of 21 is well prepared for, or whether the students have been conditioned by the system in such a way that it is very difficult for them to make this 'other type of learning' happen out of their own efforts. This is why it is more and more the aim of many adult education institutions to incorporate some 'Learning how to Learn as an Adult' into their courses. The world-wide Waldorf School Movement is an example of an education that prepares its students well for the transition to adulthood and Adult Learning at about the age of 21. As adults, these students seem better able to continue their learning through life in an independent way. In their case, the change happens almost naturally. This process of change must be imagined to happen mainly between the ages of 18 and 21. But if, after the age of 21, in professional training institutions such as universities, *child-type* school learning continues, which is very often the case, that school type of learning becomes fixed and remains for the rest of life.

In the opinion of the author, many of these institutions are not yet pursuing *adult* education but continuing *child* school education. One main reason lies in the fact that many excellent experts, artists and scientists are appointed university teachers without ever having been schooled for the profession of adult educator. It is assumed that, if people are experts, they will automatically be good adult educators as well. This, unfortunately, is not so in most cases. However, the longer the child school type of learning continues into adulthood, the stronger will be the deformation inflicted by the system of education!

12.2. The Organization

Apart from our education, the organization or community we work for or live in has a strongly formative influence. Often during management courses the author was able to tell whether somebody was a 'Shell person', an 'IBMer', working for Ford, a typical banker, insurance agent or civil servant. The question is: How is it possible that the forces working within a work context can have such a strong effect that they become outwardly visible? Are we still individuals, or have we become already 'organization persons'? The combination of variables at work here is complex and diverse. There are, for instance, those coming from the *product*, those connected with the *function* we have, or those connected with the *'culture'* of the organization.

Product: Bank functionaries behave quite differently from the way people do in the computer business, in the chemical industry or in mechanical engineering. The oil industry, coal-mining, diamond or gold mining—each have a fundamentally different influence on people. The atmosphere in a sawmill is quite different from that in a weavery, and so on.

Function: There is a well-known difference between line and staff management, between headquarters and branch offices, also between accounting departments, sales, production, administration and departments for human resources and development. They require different ways of thinking and behaving, specific skills. Also, it has a decisive effect whether we do planning, implementing or control work. The increasing division of labour regiments our possibility of learning. The exaggerated specialization of work may lead to a psychological specialization as well.

Culture: Every organization has its own identity, its explicit or implicit principles and required way of behaving. If we want to work in such a culture, we have to adapt to it and identify with it in all its nuances. Also, we must not forget that there are numerous in-service courses serving the purpose of reinforcing the organization and thus also its culture. Consider, moreover, that in modern organizational teaching, the organization itself is regarded as a continual learning system. It then becomes obvious that these influences may have a considerable formative effect on adults that might lead to a fixation. In the latter case, the term 'organizational deformation' can be used. Innumerable executives have had to realize that it has become next to impossible for them to transfer to a different type of organizational culture. We are dealing, here, with a struggle between ego and organization, individual and community. At first, this organizational learning, according to our destiny, can often be very enriching, because we can gain much valuable experience. Then, however, a time may come when all that learning has become habitual, has become fixed patterns of thinking and acting. As a result, we are no longer able to behave in a different way.

With our biography, the critical point is around the age of 35, in the mid-life stage. It is around this time that it is determined whether we become an organization person or remain an individual able creatively to participate in the continual renewal of the company. This problem comes to expression in the well-known 'resistance to change'. Up to the age of 35 most people remain flexible enough to be retrained, but after that it often becomes a problem. Therefore, regarding their in-service education, the companies are faced with the task of developing creative people for the *future.* Unfortunately, however, what is still being done, in most cases, is to train and condition personnel to conform to the *present* company. For a better understanding it should be mentioned that, here, the term 'organization' refers to all types of work communities. This is why this process starts already after puberty (around the age of 14), when adolescents begin to wrestle with conflicts between their individuality and their environment. This struggle lasts from 14 to 35, which is to say, a period of 21 years, with the crucial point of change lying around the age of 35. Then it is determined whether we have identified ourselves totally with our work community or are able to maintain some inner freedom as a creative resource. The former case is an example of organizational deformation. *Outer* adaptation to the organization, which is often necessary, does not necessarily mean *inner* adaptation.

12.3. The Profession

Personality-forming forces are strongest mainly with the self-employed professions, such as doctors, artists, lawyers, consultants, priests and so on. If we have practised them for the larger part of our life, and if we have become really expert in our subject—which often takes a long time—and yet stay creative, we are recognized by our colleagues as a *professional,* an *authority.* Someone who starts to repeat themselves and works out of routine, is no longer recognized as a professional. Likewise, someone who has not been practising for a time, is no longer recognized as a colleague. As a consequence, the tendency to over-identify with their profession emerges. Actually, they are no longer *pursuing* a profession—they have *become* it. This is when professional development turns into professional deformation. Some examples:

1. The teachers who can never be brief during meetings, but behave as if it were part of a lesson with their class. They seem prisoners of their own talking. Also, they may develop a didactic attitude and always be 'teaching' in whatever situation they may be.
2. The consultant who always knows better and advises everybody how best to do things, often hiding behind this style.
3. The minister of religion who overemphasizes a moral element in any social situation.
4. With visual arts practitioners, often there emerges an aversion to look at situations in an objective factual way. The preference is to stick to artistic experience. Artistic perception of everything becomes dominant.
5. The acquired professionality of civil, or public, servants accurately to interpret the law in every situation, can become a deformation when asked to make quick, improvized decisions in the face of natural disasters.
6. Adult educators, because they think it might show their incapability, could become so that they are hardly able to bear *not* helping someone. This often leads to inner stress and wrong decisions.
7. The manager might use a 'will language': short, quick, factual, abbreviated, where only the most essential is expressed. This can lead to an atrophy of the ability to deal with, for example, considerations about the consequences of certain decisions, moral issues and deciding between basic alternatives. Many managers have become outwardly directed pragmatists, who neglect their inner life.

These few examples might be sufficient to characterize professional deformation. Professional deformation, therefore, means that the personality and what is done professionally have become identical. In this respect, the decisive time in a person's biography is fairly late, around 49 years of age. The problem starts already around 28 when we become more and more of a specialist in our profession, really becoming expert in only a limited field. In this phase—between 28 and 35—it still contributes much to our development. Between 35 and 42, the individual and the profession are more or less in balance. From 42 onwards, however, we are tempted to keep improving what we can do well—or to avoid at all costs what we cannot do so well, because it creates insecurity and fear. Thus, the forties turn into a continuous, half-conscious battle of prestige between inner inadequacies and outer success. The specialists—doctors, accountants, priests, civil servants, etc.—must not make any mistakes and constantly have to prove to the world that they are professionally 'perfect'. Thus, around the age of 50, they are for ever repeating themselves in a limited field. There is still room for improvement in what they can do, but not for anything fundamentally new.

The remedy lies in the possibility of giving up part of our proven skills to create an inner space that will allow us to stay creative. New questions, new areas, have to be opened up. Awakening to the present and the future needs of the world around us challenges us to develop new talents. This allows us to stay creative and overcome professional deformation. It means that learning in the second half of life takes on a different character, arising as it does from a different stage in our biography. As our vitality is no longer as fresh and youthful, a stronger spiritual incentive is demanded to awaken our will to learn.

At the age of 49, then, we have reached the critical point when our professional faculties either become an impediment or may be transformed. 'How to stay creative?' becomes the dominant question for professional people in the last period of their lives.

In conclusion:

0—21:   From child school learning to Adult Learning. It manifests as an ego crisis.

14—35:   Community building and individual development. It manifests as a psychological crisis.

28—49:   From professional development to the creative person. It manifests as a spiritual crisis.

This is depicted graphically in Diagram 9.

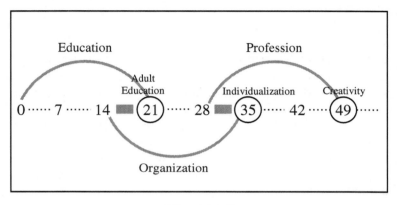

Diagram 9

The Diagram shows that between 14–21 and 28–35 the periods overlap. This means that already from 14 onwards, school education should prepare the students for Adult Learning. The period between 28–35 is a little more complicated. This is because it is the time when Adult Learning capacities have been achieved, and it coincides with the beginning of 'professionalization', under the influence of all the organizational variables. No wonder that this period of life up to the 42nd year of life is called the time of the mid-life crisis in men and women. Very specific adult education programmes could be beneficial here. They should be concerned with the *tensions* existing between the individual and the community, the individual and the family, the individual and the profession (vocation, in the true sense), and with developing *new forces* to deal with them. Learning, here, means to learn from the way we deal with the conditions of life.

Whatever form our education may take up to 21 years of age, we are endowed with certain strengths and weaknesses. Destiny unfolds out of what we have brought with us and what we encounter. Therefore, every person enters adult-hood with certain strengths and weaknesses, possibilities and impossibilities. The demands made by destiny become visible, the learning tasks in life become apparent.

In the second period, from 14 to 35, we are given the opportunity to learn through the *outer demands* that are made on us and by coping with the *inner weaknesses*. Regarding Destiny Learning, these are very important circumstances. This is because, out of our confrontation with life, the weaknesses may be transformed into strengths, that is to say into new faculties. In those areas in which we are particularly underdeveloped, the greatest change may be achieved by way of learning through destiny. During this learning process, it is possible to discover the sense and the task of our personal destiny. The above-mentioned adult education courses in the middle years could be dedicated to this learning objective.

Therefore the period from 28 to 49, in particular the for-ties, may serve the purpose of transforming the inadequacies caused by destiny. Through our life experiences, the weak-nesses we have brought with us have now been turned into new strengths. They are experienced as talents we have acquired ourselves and not those simply brought with us. Talents, as such, often hinder the person's development. An overemphasized intellect may lead to a lack of feeling, while a rich emotional disposition may lead to weak thinking, etc.

As already mentioned, whatever we have achieved through Destiny Learning should, after 49, selflessly be made avail-able to others instead of being held on to as personal property.

Concerning the vocation of the adult educator, part of our own Destiny Learning could mean changing from being the capable teaching expert to becoming a helping friend.

12.4. The Seven Learning Processes in Our Biography

So far we have found that Adult Learning can both be sup-ported as well as hindered by the influences exerted by our education, the organization we work for and our profession.

In what ways do the life phases themselves affect our learning processes? It is well known that people learn in a different way at each stage of their life, and that each of those stages offers different learning capacities.

One starting point is that, approximately from the age of 21, our ego has to transform the Seven Life Processes into learning processes. How does this happen between 21 and 28, how between 28 and 35, how between 35 and 42, and so on? Spiritual science describes human soul development in these three phases in the following way:

21 to 28:   Development of the sentient soul;
28 to 35:   Development of the intellectual/mind soul;
35 to 42:   Development of the consciousness soul.

As there is an extensive literature available on the subject, this will not be developed further here, except to look at how it relates to Adult Learning.[9]

From 21 to 28 Years of Age:

In this period, the sentient soul supports, even reinforces, the first two learning processes of breathing and warming. We yearn to take in something new. Real life offers itself as a thrilling adventure; we are easily filled with enthusiasm or disappointed. There is a great need to breathe in something new and to unite with it on a feeling level. The first two learning processes are emphasized by the sentient soul. This happens at a time in life when adult education is very common. The learning process should make use of this disposition and strengthen it to such an extent that it can carry through the other five learning processes to reach the creativity in the seventh and last learning process.

From 28 to 35 Years of Age:

The mind soul is more inward; it assimilates and individualizes, thereby reinforcing the middle three learning processes: *digesting, individualizing, practising*. It may serve the purpose of thoroughly and consciously working through what has been taken in. Agreeing, disagreeing, doubting, checking, confronting with different points of view, all of these are activities the mind soul is familiar with. It is true that the individualizing process in Step 4 is a deed of the ego, but it is supported by the mind soul, the actual middle part of the human soul. The period from 28 to 35 is the middle of life. It is a time in which the human being is most balanced, and is learning to develop some inner certainty by establishing a congruence between inner world and outer world. However, it is also an age at which many people sink into a life of mere routine by repeating dutifully certain thought patterns, modes of behaviour and will activities. Being able to practise in a conscious, systematic, investigating way is a gift of the mind soul. The danger is mindless repetition of what we have learned!

Therefore, the mind soul in particular can support the middle learning processes of digesting, individualizing and practising. If, on the one hand, this builds on the first two processes, and on the other, is strong enough to allow new growth of faculties to enable us to externalize in an original way what has been learned, the whole learning process is thereby accomplished.

From 35 to 42 Years of Age:

In this period of life the supporting energy of our life forces, our vitality, in our life processes is beginning to diminish in a biological sense and needs to be replaced by a stronger involvement of our ego forces. This supports the translation of life processes into learning processes—but only if the ego in its learning activity makes use of this biological situation to let new faculties grow and use the transformed life-forces in a creative way.

Diminishing biological vitality leads either to physical decay or to new spiritual vitality; either to physical dependence or to spiritual awakening. The danger in this period is that the consciousness soul might receive too little from the first two previous learning processes: observation and warming enthusiasm. Characteristic barrenness, void, loneliness, boredom and inner helplessness begin to show. We become less capable of activating ourselves from within by our own ego efforts, but need increasingly to be stimulated from outside.

Often, in adult education learning processes, strong measures and learning activities have to be used to help people engage again in an independent, investigating way of learning. However, much more is possible in this respect than is generally assumed.

From 42 to 49 Years of Age:

The previous periods have led to open questions requiring a new faculty to observe, stronger enthusiasm, a more careful digesting process, etc. Unlike the previous three periods of life that were still supported by human soul development, more effort is now needed for everything. Destiny, however, remains our helper! The author has met many people who, due to extraordinary and often unexpected events, started developing again; but, only if they accepted these 'interferences' as meaningful for their path of learning from destiny. If we do this, we can then understand the interferences from a different perspective and be warmed from a different source.

From 49 to 56 Years of Age:

While the mirroring, corresponding period from 28 to 35 mainly served the purpose of individualizing the learning process, the emphasis is now on growing new faculties, thereby enabling us to become creative again. (See Diagram 10.)

We are born into this world with many dormant talents that we have not acquired but which are simply there. While a part of them is unfolded and activated through our education, because it is not challenged by the environment, another part remains dormant. In adult life, further talents are challenged, awoken, promoted and activated by the profession, the work community, our destiny. We keep learning all the time. At the age of 49 we have acquired many talents and skills and have experienced a great deal. It seems as if we have exhausted all

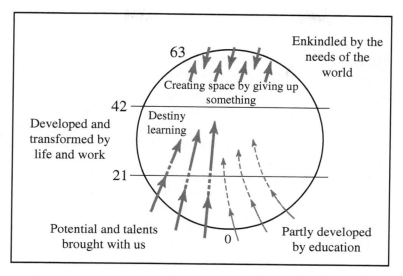

Diagram 10

our possibilities. Further development now depends on a kind of sacrifice, entailing renunciation. We have to be able to give up something of what we have achieved to create an inner space. This is so that we can discover something new, in the form of an unresolved question in the world we meet. There are innumerable situations of this kind that involve hidden questions. With traditional skills and knowledge, they can be neither comprehended nor solved. To be able to perceive these needs of the world, is the beginning of a new learning process that may develop new faculties. Just as in the period of 28 to 35 a rather egocentric learning process took place, so in the fifties an altruistic learning process may begin. These new faculties are self-acquired, not simply brought with us and then developed. Sometimes they are talents from another area that have been metamorphosed. A musical talent may metamorphose into a social ability; an entrepreneurial ability into a more spiritual initiative force. This biographical transition is the source of creativity in the latter part of life. It is significant that the fifties have been described as the most creative age of the human being.

From 56 to 63 years of age:

Because we become increasingly independent of the influence of our bodily organism, the spiritual up-building becomes increasingly possible. The outward creativity then results from an inner rejuvenation. In this way the Seven Learning Processes may be extended over our whole lifetime. Indeed, our biography can show itself to be a learning, changing system of development in itself. Destiny Learning becomes a life experience.

Particularly in the sixties, the review and evaluation of our life history is a wonderful learning process that may shed new light on all our experiences. The most unpleasant in particular, as well as the most joyful events, may prove to be of great significance for our Destiny Learning.

The curriculum of our learning biography is a work of art by far surpassing the best university in the world. This is why the attempt is being made here to show the connection between our biography and our learning. It may also serve the adult educator as an example of how to create learning situations that support people's 'Learning through Life'. Our learning seems to include spiritual development when our ego keeps on striving to grow and become, enhancing our third basic drive for perfection, to do everything better and better (as mentioned in Chapter 1).

It will be obvious that in our seventies, eighties and nineties learning is less and less body-bound, with the Seven Learning Processes often happening almost simultaneously. The fruits of the past are harvested, and seeds are sown for the future. This is how the Seven Learning Processes are part of our biography. With the help of the powers of destiny, they may lead to Learning through Life. In the following section the Sevenfold Learning Process in Destiny Learning is described.

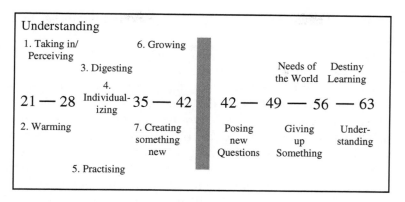

Diagram 11

12.5 The Sevenfold Learning Process in Destiny Learning

During the preparation of the present book, Destiny Learning, as an aspect of Adult Learning, has enjoyed a rapid development: its didactic, its supporting exercises, special courses and workshops and specific applications to other fields, such as art therapy, counselling, consulting, etc. A schooling for Destiny Learning Facilitators is now available.

How to work with these processes of Destiny Learning is already being applied in some biography courses, with titles such as 'From Biography to Karma', in 'karma courses' as well as in the 'Schooling for Biography Facilitators and Counsellors' as developed in several places in Europe. Moreover, this learning process is a basis for the schooling of people wanting to do 'biography work', that is to say, wanting to help people understand and cope with their destiny.

The author is preparing a further book that will develop in more detail the Adult Learning aspect of Destiny Learning. What is offered here, then, should be seen as only an introduction. It is included for the sake of showing how the three aspects of Adult Learning ('School/Earthly Learning', 'Destiny Learning' and 'Spiritual Research') form an integrated, interweaving whole, with each being based upon the

Seven Life/Learning Processes and complementing and supporting the others.

In Chapter 5 the Sevenfold Learning Process was described as a fairly organized, conscious process. However, a much more unconscious learning process has also been described. This is a process that takes place in life, guided by destiny, which, in people's biographies, often manifest as the most essential, the real process of their development. Trying to transform this way of learning through destiny and life into a conscious learning process, it soon becomes obvious that here, too, the Seven Learning Steps can be the foundation. In the following the attempt will be made to describe these Seven Steps, which, to be effective, need to be worked through assiduously.

One decisive difference from the usual learning process lies in the learning *material* which presents itself as destiny events, destiny situations, or even as our physical constitution, as a very individual quality. This means that the learning material is destiny itself, or *karma*.

A second difference is that the Seven Steps really require totally new qualities and attitudes that are normally not used in this way.

A third difference is that 'Learning how to Learn' here means to acquire ever greater freedom of choice regarding destiny. In other words, the learning objective is to deal more consciously with Learning through Life, and to speed up the process. Doing so, we learn to meet our destiny increasingly in a creative way.

12.5.1. Step One: Breathing—Perceiving a Destiny Event

At this level, we have to learn to observe destiny events; really to observe them with all our senses. This is much more difficult than with normal learning. This is because destiny approaches from outside and is met in a specific way from the inside. It belongs to the person it approaches, and immediately it triggers all sorts of reactions that need to be overcome before it becomes possible to perceive the destiny situation with the senses. There are many exercises that help us acquire this quality of learning to observe destiny as objectively as possible. One useful exercise in this regard is the *daily review* that Rudolf Steiner recommended.

Destiny manifests in events that take place outwardly, but also in what occurs inwardly during the event. One excellent method for observing at least an aspect of our destiny is where such an event is worked through meticulously. We remember an event that we sense was of significance. Every possible outer sense detail is brought into consciousness. What did it look like? What were the sounds, the smells, the temperature, etc. Then, what went on inwardly *at the time of the event*? What thoughts came up in me? What did I feel at that moment? What did I want? The event is *'breathed'* in and out, and *karma* presents itself as a learning objective. This requires the development of the ability to accept the event as a *fact*.

From this, it is clear why the daily review is really a karmic exercise. It trains us continuously to work in the way described above.

12.5.2. Step Two: Warming—Placing the Event in Our Biography

Now this event must be given a place in my present life and my biography. Biography means description of our life. The chosen event becomes consciously part of my history. It belongs to me; it is included in my life. For example, if I had an accident when I was 32, it could have been a very important moment of destiny. It has to do with an individual (me) who, in this life, met that accident, at that age, in that circumstance. Much led up to it and many consequences followed. As I bring it into consciousness in this exercise, I *'warm'* to it, I connect with it as a part of the totality of my life, my biography. The meaning may not be clear yet, but the connection with my personal development is experienced as a *warming*.

This Second Step is more inward because it has a meaning for the individual's own life. Life Learning gets much stronger, much deeper. Significant questions arise, such as:

What *quality* has the event? What *gesture* does it have? Do I recognize *similar situations* in my biography, or does it stand on its own? The destiny we meet with is 'warmed' and becomes our own concern, as the karmic composition of our biography is revealed! Any 'biography work' undertaken from the viewpoint of destiny, can support this Second Learning Step.

12.5.3. Step Three: Digesting—Discovering the Meaning of the Destiny Forces

Concerning the *'digesting'* process of this step, we need to understand that it is a meeting between:

a. What is demanded from us from outside ourselves; and,
b. How we can meet those demands with the inner resources available to us.

Destiny may favour or challenge human beings. It may bring great joy, misfortune or innumerable other circumstances. *People* meet all of this with their physical, emotional and spiritual possibilities and weaknesses. These two worlds seldom consciously blend, but for this very reason the encounter is essential. Everything depends on whether or not people are prepared fully to accept their destiny as a problem of learning through life. To do so takes a great deal of courage, for there are countless opportunities to blame and make out that other people and outer circumstances are responsible for what happens to us, or for what we can or cannot do. This, however, means that the individuals concerned do not accept what happens to them as part of the destiny that is both connected with them and asks something from them. This is why this Learning Step is often experienced as an inner wrestling for self-knowledge. When fully worked with, it results in a recognition that a clear, meaningful step in Learning through Life has been made.

A person can identify a karmic event. They might even understand it in the whole configuration of the biography. Often, however, when they start to ask themselves: what *is* it? why did it happen to *me*? they cannot avoid a strong self-confrontation. Questions arise, such as: 'Who *am* I really?' 'Why did it *have* to come to me?' 'What do I have to *do* about it?' With the step of digesting, we often need help. Some people can do it themselves, but others cannot. This is the sphere where a 'helping conversation', or counselling, might be useful.

An advantageous thought might be: 'If I were a different person, it might not have happened that way.' This is usually painful, because we realize that whatever it was that happened, did so *precisely* because we are what we are! A second question then follows: 'What forces do I need to develop, or what do I need to change in me to make this learning event unnecessary?' Or, similarly, 'Why do I need this aspect of destiny, and why do I have to go through this?'

Often, this digestion process leads to meeting what is called 'a second person in us'. We are really seeing two people: the *person* who has developed in this life, through the family, the country, the language, etc., and the *ego* from previous incarnations that pulsates in our will and practically *is* our will. Thus, in the unconscious person, lives the other person who works on from old incarnations. Aspects of this second person are discovered in the process of this Third Step, and are made manifest through our destiny situation if we have the courage to unveil what is hidden. The causes in last lives for a present destiny become apparent.

Part of our double may also become visible when we learn in this way. Also many karmic issues are discovered that have not been transformed in the past. Most psychological disorders are caused by undigested old karma. This is another reason why courage is needed to reach into this level of ourselves, and why help from other people could be of benefit.

12.5.4. Step Four: Individualizing—Accepting our Destiny
Next, the problem of Learning through Life has to be made our life task. This is something totally different from trying to solve a problem. The outer event now disappears altogether; it was merely the manifestation of what came

from past lives and the presentation of what needs to be transformed now. We have to commit ourselves to working on it in our daily life. *Individualizing* means to make a decision of will that provides both the motive and the motivating force for any further Destiny Learning.

With Destiny Learning, when we are dealing with karma forces, we see a life situation that has been prepared in the higher worlds out of the deeds and achievements of former incarnations. Again it must be mentioned that it takes courage to look at an event in this way, to unveil it in our biography and to observe at least an aspect of ourselves as we really are.

The process of this Fourth Step means to develop towards a total identification with our karma. In so far as it is related to the original event, there must eventually be a total and full identification with it. Total identification with it means an acceptance of the truth. We need to develop the understanding that: 'The only thing that I really own is my karma.' The moment when we can come to *that*, is the moment when it becomes our mission and task to take it, accept it, own it and work with it in the way it asks of us.

One of the methods that can help, is to write down what we have discovered. This is because it can very easily be forgotten. Another method that helps people to come close to this total identification, is to make a colour drawing of the second person and then consecutive drawings of what could develop out of it in the future. Sometimes, the second person is given a name, so we can carry them further as a companion.

It is important to work through thoroughly each phase of these destiny processes. It is so easy to stay in the first phases or only half digest matters. This demands very hard work as a learning process.

12.5.5. Step Five: Maintaining—Practising the Transformation in Daily Life

This step is of a nature different from the usual kind of learning, because the karmic decision of the Fourth Step will have a formative influence on our further destiny. The question now is how to find the appropriate exercises to *maintain* and foster this decision that has now become a 'task', foster it not in a structured learning situation but in everyday life itself. The destiny that is waiting for us becomes our field of *practice*; practising has to be assigned its own place in our way of living. Moreover, we may discover that life itself becomes a teacher, which gives a number of hints as to how and what to practise. Therefore, the art of this kind of Learning through Life, is to discover a new way of learning. In this respect, life itself manifests as a hidden teacher constantly offering the subject matter, learning method and learning objectives.

Now, assume that the Fourth Step has been completed and we see the task. In practice, this means that we have perceived that part of our being which must be transformed. The problem is that such pictures can disappear or be forgotten, so they need to be maintained or cared for. This caring is *practising*. In normal learning situations, we do exercises. In the karma learning process, exercising takes place in daily life. We can practise when the next event occurs, and we can recognize the same pattern happening again. The author knows a person who has worked through a situation well because of this total identification. It helped for her to make a picture and give it a name. She said: 'My picture is that of a nice little girl in me who has never grown up. It has been educated into me. I still have it, and that constitutes a burden for me.' Now, in practising, she may find herself saying something which causes her to realize: 'Ugh! there's that nice little girl with a smile again!' So she looks for a 'counter deed' as an exercise to transform gradually the nice girl into a mature person.

Carrying this identification picture within us is a precondition for practising. We face the picture repeatedly whilst a slow transformation takes place. The author has the impression that a person who takes the first four steps already influences future destiny. It is very difficult to say whether this happens because *we* recognise and work with the picture, or because our angel or the higher worlds help us, or a combination of these. In any case, it must be because the acceptance of karma as a reality is truly a *choice* in life. It is usually a shocking experience because it comes home forcibly to us that we have until now lived under an illusion. Before, we knew only the external pictures, such as the people, events and places we have seen. Even our inner way of thinking, concepts, feelings, desires, intentions, etc., tend to cover up the forces of destiny.

We need to take this very seriously. Today, this is particularly relevant to feelings, which we talk about a great deal. Do we really believe that our feelings relate only to now? No, most of our feelings come from our prebirth experiences. We have a conscious aspect, of course, but also an unconscious aspect, where most of our feeling life is really something that works on from prebirth into this life. That is the origin of most feelings. A full recognition of this is also of help when we deal with our destiny.

The will goes even further back, because the impulses living in our will come from our former incarnations.

12.5.6. Step Six: Growing—Growing the New Faculty of Karmic Perception

All of these steps will steadily lead us to the new ability, inwardly and outwardly, of observing the forces of destiny. The network of destiny forces weaving in relationships between people becomes conscious in us. Destiny in the past, present and future may be understood as a process of development. We begin to experience the reality of the forces of karma that are manifesting in life but which are, at the same time, highly spiritual.

Often, when a number of events has been worked through along the lines of the first five steps just described, just as in a normal learning process, they start to connect, interpenetrate, form a symbiosis. The process of this Sixth Step, finally transforms into a new faculty of the heart. This has to do with an increasing awareness of the forces of destiny: the 'karma sense'.

It becomes clear that the aim of Destiny Learning is not

primarily to solve problems, but rather it is to do with transforming past destiny into future faculties. It is a total life process, a Life Learning. This is done by perceiving that destiny forces are observed from the heart and not from the head. Therefore, Destiny Learning means increasing aware-ness of how we meet every situation anew, but also with growing consciousness of how we want to transform our destiny. This increased awareness of destiny appears in a larger context, and begins to connect more and more with other people's destinies. We begin to sense a network, and move slowly from our individual karma to a perception that it all has to do with a far greater interweaving of karma that *grows,* ultimately, to encompass the whole of humanity.

The so-called negative aspects in our karma are really the greatest opportunities for the future; that is why they are there! All this comes from the growing awareness of the social dimension of destiny learning.

12.5.7. Step Seven: Reproducing—Bringing Order to One's Destiny

The culmination of the six previous steps is the growing possibility of dealing creatively with destiny situations. This means intervening, in a healing and harmonizing way, within a gradually developing sphere of freedom. Destiny Learning manifests as the real, essential learning. It is the basis of any other kind of learning described so far. It has human beings themselves as the starting point. For is not every learning situation a kind of encounter caused by destiny? Moreover, we notice that this learning process starts in a very personal way in order later to reveal itself ever increasingly as a net-work of destiny that involves more and more people.

In spiritual science, many exercises are given that can be used to support these Seven Learning Steps. For instance:

— The daily retrospective review;
— The 'second human being' within us;
— The 'four-day karma exercise' and the threefold manifestation of life before birth;

— The so-called 'three-level exercise';
— Observation exercises, etc.[10]

As we move through the previous six steps, the ability of karmic perception increases more and more. As this happens, we gain a much more objective relationship to our karma. This can go so far that the margin of choice for future deeds increases and we can become *creative* in them.

It is important to realize that Destiny Learning has quite a different aim from the normal learning process, where we learn to understand, for instance, how to read a balance-sheet as a specialist faculty. With Destiny Learning, also, we have developed a new, very special faculty: a faculty to perceive the threads of the karmic network that weaves between people. By working through our own destiny, this ability grows, and the more it grows, the more of a margin of freedom emerges. This is the Seventh Step: the bringing into being of a creative relationship to destiny.

This Path of Learning also does justice to the second of the drives mentioned in Chapter 1, the *drive for development*, which, after all, is based on a learning process aimed at assimilating destiny.

Another kind of Destiny Learning takes place when adult educators look back on their own education to find new forms of learning, as described in Chapter 15.

In summary, it may be said that Destiny Learning can be regarded as the starting point of all learning processes. It fructifies, deepens, and humanizes the usual school type of learning which is often out of touch with life. Moreover it is the starting point of the Spiritual Schooling Path.

Part Three:
Practical Applications

13. Learning How to Learn

Many adult education institutions have found that most people are quite unprepared for the kind of learning appropriate for adults that is described in this book. They often demand more school-like forms, academic systems or total freedom. All this virtually abolishes the adult educator. This has led to the opinion that adult education should always start by teaching people how to learn in an adult way, including dealing with learning blockages.

Blockages in Adult Learning may be due to many reasons.

1. To a large extent they are due to damage inflicted by the outside world during childhood, while the person was going to school or university, or during the education itself. Here, people are taught methods, characteristics, attitudes and habits that may have a hindering or conditioning effect.

   Anyway, the transition from child learning to Adult Learning is a step that has far-reaching consequences; and there are innumerable adults who have never, or only partly, made this step. What is necessary in our times is a thorough analysis of our own learning faculties and blockages, as well as specific methods to overcome the latter.

2. A second category has to do with the inner nature of the human being. Our dispositions are very different. In most of us, soul forces are either underdeveloped or over-emphasized. In this respect, we ought to consider the Spiritual Schooling Path (the third Path of Learning) to keep developing our possibilities of a being capable of learning and acquiring knowledge and insight.

   In the following, a method is described for discovering learning hindrances. Moreover, indications important both for the adult educator and the adult learner are given on how to overcome these hindrances.

There are innumerable learning blockages; too many to list them all. Therefore, just a few are given for each of the Seven Learning Steps—hopefully enough to enable the reader then to undertake his or her own research. Also, only a few possible measures for remedial exercises are presented—hopefully enough to find the specific measures appropriate in each case. The following blockages have been described by colleagues interviewed about these problems.

13.1. The Seven Learning Steps as a Diagnosis for Learning Hindrances

13.1.1. Observing—Taking-in

In general, we can say that wherever our twelve senses are dulled in any way, a barrier to learning will result. Our observational capacity constitutes the way in to all learning! The capacity of the ego actively to engage all of our 12 senses in *observation* becomes our learning strength.

Blockages:

— Setting the warming, or digestive, process in motion at the 'observing' stage;
— Willing, or being able, to take in nothing but precisely defined concepts;
— Willing, or being able, to take in nothing but pictures;
— Being able or willing to take in only according to a specific learning model;
— Being able to think only in words;
—·Not hearing what is really meant;
— Taking in with immediate criticism or strong prejudices;
— General aversion to lectures, instructions, descriptions;
— Desire for lectures, instructions, descriptions;
— Aversion to authority;
— Desire for authority;
— Aversion to statements;
— Need for statements;
— Passive way of taking in;
— Emotional way of taking in, etc., etc.

Solutions:

It is obvious that our egoism will sneak into 'taking in'. While the senses are selfless, our ego is not. Proper breathing, as well as proper observation, has to become selfless breathing. This is why fostering a basic attitude of openness, wonder, amazement and reverence has a healing effect on the process of perception. Similarly, any exercise that enlivens the activity of the senses. The many exercises that enhance objective visual and auditory observation can support the learner here.

13.1.2. Warming—Relating/Connecting

Basically, our *warmth body* determines with what and in which way we can relate to the learning content that enters our system through the senses. Warming is relating to and connecting. Some elements can be experienced as abstract and cold, others are familiar and warm, others incomprehensible, others exciting, etc., etc. This warming and cooling process, highly differentiated in endless variations, establishes our ability to connect with all that presents itself as learning material through our senses.

Generally, it can be said that whenever the ego is incapable of becoming active inwardly, the process of learning lacks motivation and is therefore lamed. The ego has to be able to produce warmth out of itself by means of maintaining an active, deep and enthusiastic interest in what it has chosen to be focused on.

Blockages:

— Indifference; inability to be 'moved';
— Lack of imagination (imagination is required to foster interest);
— Not making a connection unless something is presented in 'my' particular way;
— I am only interested in certain things;
— 'Know it already!', 'Have heard it before!' (Too many stimuli);
— Over-enthusiasm, etc., etc.

Solutions:

All disorders here are due to irregularities in the relationship between the inner and outer worlds. This takes place mainly in our feeling life. Therefore, any exercise enabling our ego to intervene in an active (warming-cooling) and regulating way, will reinforce the learning process. This is decisive for the first three steps of learning, because it is solely the warmth of the ego that turns an observation into a meaningful perception, overcomes emotional disorders, and provides energy for the digesting process.

13.1.3. Digesting—Assimilating

Generally, it can be said that our tendency to 'take it easy' and the inclination to be comfortable, will repeatedly tempt our spirit to become lazy. We will invest much energy in physical well-being, but very little in our spiritual well-being. Thus, a kind of mental entropy is the biggest barrier to the process of digestion. A large amount of content sinks into our organism undigested, where it may cause both nervous and metabolic disorders.

Blockages:

— Passive taking in of learning material;
— Tendency to learn in an easy way;
— Mental laziness;
— Too earth-bound in our body;
— Digesting only intellectually;
— Digesting only emotionally;
— Fear of having to face consequences;
— Fear of destroying the learning content;
— Fear of new things that could dislodge our present convictions;
— Fear of embarrassing questions coming up;
— Belief in authority;
— Lack of self-confidence, etc., etc.

Solutions:

Digesting learning content means testing our courage to overcome our fear of learning independently. Therefore, any activity that encourages our will to know and understand is of the greatest importance here. What must be considered is that all three forces of the soul—thinking, feeling and will— will be involved in the process of assimilation and digesting, not just our thinking. The digestion process serves to help, find and experience the essential, the meaningful, instead of merely assembling information. Countless exercises are available for this purpose:

— Confronting the new learning with past experiences;
— Trying to think the opposite of what we have taken in;
— Finding concrete examples from practical life;
— Expressing in an artistic way what we have taken in;
— Assessing, judging and questioning the new learning, etc.
— We can digest in *thinking* by trying to understand; in *feeling* by awakening our sense of truth; in *will* by trying things out.

In conclusion, it may be said that in practising these first three learning processes, the learning adult is practising to become an independent self-learner. The drive to acquire knowledge and real understanding is awakened. People then learn to take in the world with clear observation. They learn to relate personally to what was observed. Finally, in Step Three, they learn to work it through in such a way that it may become entirely their own possession.

13.1.4. Individualizing
Generally, taking this step in a conscious way leads to the experience of an inner abyss, which is also called a threshold experience. The disappearance of something old and the birth of something new is always experienced as a void, a zero-point. Many people wish to avoid this shock. Therefore, these moments of individualizing represent fairly unexpected

breakthroughs. The main barrier is the instinctive avoidance of this experience. Many learning processes skip this event of individualizing, thereby bypassing true Adult Learning. Some of the blockages are:

Blockages:

— Fear of the abyss (threshold);
— The opinion that we cannot know anything out of ourselves with certainty. We have to believe (religious authority) or follow the scientifically agreed method (scientific authority), or the judgement of an expert (personal authority). In each case the individualizing of the learning process does not happen and an imitation process appears in its place;
— Being habituated to an 'answer-culture' (information) instead of a 'question-culture'. According to the former attitude, learning should always be repeatable or capable of being imitated. Examinations are often based on this principle. This means, however, that the basic, individual moment in learning is excluded; then it is almost impossible to merge the drive for knowledge with the drive to develop;
— If learning, developing, and gaining knowledge and insight are regarded as a continuous process, then a permanent uncertainty is involved, for we are continuously changing. If the ego is unable to live with this, and does not experience that it fosters the greatest creativity, then the process of individualizing our learning is seriously blocked;
— Changing and developing is a constant process of self-confrontation. Many people try to avoid precisely this, and it constitutes a powerful barrier to learning.

Solutions:

If adult educators are able to bring about situations in which the learners may experience that a new inner security is created by their very own, fiery ego will—an activity that dissolves all fears and insecurities into nothingness—then, precisely here, the most secure ground is laid for Adult Learning. By our own activity the drive to gain knowledge and insight and the drive to develop become identical. There is no 'recipe' of how to do this since this process is different for every human being and is deeply connected with our destiny. In the individualizing process, everyday learning and Destiny Learning are combined. What is also helpful is:

— To foster an attitude that wants to find real questions and live with them, rather than assemble informative answers that close off our own searching;
— To show the deepest respect for the individual learning event;
— To aim towards reducing the old veneration for 'content'. Then, instead of being an end in itself, 'content' will become a means for learning and developing. Thus we can become more of a human being.

13.1.5. Maintaining—Practising/Exercising

The transition from the 'breakthrough' to the careful, meticulous practising of exercises, is quite hard to deal with. An inner discipline is now required. This is why there are often deeply hidden barriers to this learning activity. In earlier times, regular praying or meditating was a common thing to do. Nowadays, with our restless, hectic style of living, it has become a necessity of life. Many adult educators complain about the participants' inability to carry out precise regular exercising. It appears as a laming of the will. The ego must learn to live in rhythms!

Blockages:

— Some participants cannot bear doing an exercise exactly as prescribed. They can only practise if the exercise is adjusted *to their own habits*;
— They are unable to feel love for what they are doing;
— They cannot perform regular, rhythmic activities;
— They have a need for immediate results. This is incompatible with patiently waiting for results;

— A general paralysis of the will. The will is paralysed due to the resistance experienced when practising and living in a technical age;
— Damage done to the participants in their youth by strict regimentation by parents and/or a harsh school discipline. This can lead to an aversion for exercising at all;
— There is a lack of the concentration required for the exercise. Being distracted easily is also a barrier to learning.

Solutions:

Generally, it can be said that:

— In adult education the motivation to practise must be born out of the Fourth Step, which is individualizing. The new shoot has to be cared for so that it can be kept alive;
— The meaning of the exercise, the 'whys and wherefors', needs to be explained as well as possible;
— The exercise needs to be based on an archetypal image to be able to grow into an ability. It is better to start with simple, comprehensible, small, attainable steps to establish a 'culture' of practising. This has to be done with love and enthusiasm. In Chapter 10 we have already considered designing and implementing exercises.

13.1.6. The Growing of New Faculties

As a rule, trained, automatic behaviour and fixed thought patterns are the biggest blockages, both to growth and creativity. In the second half of a person's life this is even further increased because of the decline in life-forces that may show as a kind of sclerosis. In old age this manifests in the declining ability to learn new things.

A response to new questions is that the ego must learn to give up the use of old talents to make space for new talents to grow.

Blockages:

— The habit of getting stuck in routines prevents the metamorphosis into new faculties;

— Also, the security of fixed ideas and opinions on what is 'right' and 'wrong' will weaken the life-forces;

— The inability to evaluate learning activities in thinking, experiencing or doing;

— The impatience of not letting previous learning processes mature quietly in our unconscious;

— Our culture is characterized by a pragmatic attitude, asking for quick, effective results. This is in conflict with letting new faculties mature quietly.

Solutions:

All educational measures that can help to awaken our drive to improve. 'Improvement' is not achieved by endless repetition but by doing the same thing in different ways. Endless variations of all learning activities will allow new faculties to grow in us.

Anything that contributes to improving the *evaluation* of learning activities will both speed up and deepen them as well. Reviewing our learning process daily contributes a great deal to 'Learning how to Learn'. Possible questions are: What have I learned today? How did it happen? What new questions have arisen in me? This would help considerably to shorten the usual long courses. Just as in the Fifth Step (practising) the adult educator has to consider motivation, explanation and objective, so here, the participants must learn to accompany and reinforce their own learning process by regularly evaluating it.

13.1.7. The Creative Learning Process

Creating something always has the character of a deed. It is a leap into the unknown, initiating something in the world that was not there before. What is used here is the initiating will, awakened by the ego. Adult education has to do with the awakening of the will, and anything in this sense that resists this initiating will is a blockage to learning. For instance, the ego here has to learn to transform and metamorphose its inner world, to be creative in the outer world.

Blockages:

— Wanting to be perfect;
— Being afraid of making mistakes;
— Wanting to engage only in predictable activities;
— A lack of self-confidence;
— A hardening of the life-forces;
— Unwillingness to take risks;
— Fear of the consequences of our 'creative' deeds, etc., etc.

Solutions:

To become a creative human being is a potential inherent in all people. It is also the aim of all Adult Learning Processes. Creativity manifests in people's actions. Its origin, however, is in the human middle, in the beating, feeling heart. This is where the first six learning processes are integrated by the last one into a higher entity. By awakening our drive for knowledge and insight, our drive to develop, and our drive to improve, we become a creative human being. This is what initiates the future.

It is difficult to say how to do this in practice because it brings into manifestation all the previous activities. However, the following exercise has proved to be quite helpful:

1. Undergo a simple learning process;
2. Closely observe and evaluate the Seven Steps you went through;
3. Then make a careful note of the (most serious) blockages;
4. From this develop a realistic plan for improvement;
5. Find the most suitable exercises for this;
6. Practise them regularly;
7. Enjoy the constant increase of your learning ability!

To seek the assistance of a (good) adult educator in this respect might be sensible.

A practical help in diagnosing our own strengths and weaknesses, after studying the above, is to evaluate them by giving them a number between 1 and 10. 10 is the learning process we are best at; 1 is the weakest; with the others in between. This gives us an overview and teaches us that by improving the weakest ones we strengthen the others.

In an institution for curative education, a modelling exercise was carefully carried through, using the Seven Processes. A diagnosis of the learning abilities of the participants was provided by noting down their strengths and weaknesses discovered on the way. Doing something similar would be another possibility.

In the long run, these Seven Steps may be transformed into a Spiritual Schooling Path.

13.2. The Learning Diary

This method of learning was first applied by adult educators wanting to improve their didactic faculties. For this purpose they took notes after each presentation of whatever had gone well and why, as well as whatever did not work so well and why not. In doing so they soon made two important discoveries:

1. That this review, this looking back from a distance, made them discover an amazing number of hitherto hidden aspects;
2. That they had missed a vast number of learning possibilities in their professional life, because they had neglected this learning by reviewing.

These two experiences then led to the development of a particular method of 'Learning how to Learn'. It was first tested in a course for adult educators and soon introduced as a method for every participant. The aim is to discover and promote our own process of learning. The participants are given a certain amount of time at the end of each day when they can review their own learning process by themselves and make a note in their diary of the most important learning events.

— At first, the main thing is to discover and note down the 'Aha!' events (moments of, perhaps startling, enlightenment, insight, *knowing*), and focus on the learning process we have gone through. This in itself enriches and deepens considerably. Also, it will help us to realize how many seemingly unrelated aspects are involved in such moments of insight, with whom or what we have come into contact, the order in which things happened, what we take in and what we do not. This leads to an initial sense of Destiny Learning.

— Soon, however, the process is greatly deepened if we write down, in addition to what we have learned, *how* this has happened. Outer observation will then gradually turn into self-observation. The question we ask is not just: *What* have I learned? but also: *How* did I learn it? and, Who *am* I as a learner?

Previously we will have done the sevenfold learning diagnosis a few times, as described above. This provides us with a main connecting thread with the help of which this semi-conscious process of learning may be examined in more detail. We need to include all those *feelings* in this second part that occurred during the learning process. They often prove to be important indications of how this learning has taken place in us. Thus, some self-knowledge is added to our normal learning.

— Keeping a diary may lead to yet a third element if we examine the consequences of the first two steps. This learning, this coming to know oneself, may raise further questions, which must quickly be jotted down. Even a decision may present itself. Every learning process is leading up to something, has certain consequences, demands a next step. In order not to let this step be superficial, some effort is needed, just as the second step requires a degree of honesty, and the first a degree of attentiveness.

A possible negative aspect of this method is the danger of over-intellectualizing. It is easy to write down long lists of learning factors. It is better, however, to choose just one or two of the most important ones. At the same time looking thoroughly into whether or not this was truly learning something new. A deeper understanding of something we knew before is also something new; it can also be qualitatively a new experience.

A second danger is that of projecting outwards the rising feelings and experiences of the second step, instead of seeing them objectively as our own. This is also why it is better not to spend too much time on the diary; 15 to 20 minutes a day is enough. It is not meant to be a detailed description of everything we have experienced, but a small part of 'Learning how to Learn'. Keeping such a diary is an exercise in itself that needs to be learned. At first, it is desirable to reserve time and space in the programme for this purpose. The exercise needs to be prepared well because it is difficult for the participants to make the transition to observing their own learning process. If it is already planned for and feasible, these discoveries may then be shared among each other. Once they have become used to it, many participants prefer to make their diary notes by themselves at home. This promotes their independence.

What is very positive is the experience that keeping this diary considerably increases the 'Learning how to Learn'; moreover, the participants' responsibility for their own learning process grows. It is highly recommended that the adult educators themselves should also take part in the exercise, giving examples to the participants if necessary. Some adult educators accompany these three steps with the following three questions:

1. What is the most important thing I have learned today?
2. How did this learning process take place in me?
3. Has it awakened a new question or intention in me?

14. Forming Judgements

The ability to form independent judgements was mentioned earlier as one of the main aims of modern adult education. Often, when intellectualism is being overemphasized, this is understood to mean a cognitive judgement only. This ignores the fact that aesthetic and moral judgements are at least as important as the cognitive judgement process. Therefore, it is most important in adult education that all three should be developed simultaneously in a harmonious way. This can increase the independence of our judgement process considerably. What do the three have in common, and what is the difference between them?

The three processes of forming a judgement are described in detail in F.W. Zeylmans van Emmichoven's book *The Anthroposophical Understanding of the Human Soul.*[11] Here, only a brief summary will be given. Judgement is a discerning and recognizing activity. The *experiencing* soul has its origin in the will life; in feeling it is a product. The *judging* soul, on the other hand, starts in the feeling life and comes to a conclusion as a product. In experiencing, the feeling reaches inwards; in judging it reaches outwards.

14.1. Forming a Cognitive Judgement

To form a clear judgement, the experiencing soul has to 'extinguish' itself, as far as possible giving up its own existence, so that the truth of the phenomenon may reveal itself. Then ego and sense world are opposite each other, undisturbed. Truth is the highest criterion. The problem that presents itself here, in the learning process, is the thinking barrier; it may be overcome with the help of the learning path.

14.2. Forming an Aesthetic Judgement

To form a clear judgement in the aesthetic area, both the experiencing soul and the judging soul are needed. The balance between the two leads to aesthetic judgement. Since this comes about at the boundary between soul and sense world, it is to be regarded as a continual process. Aesthetic judgements stem from a process of weaving between inner and outer world. If the experiencing soul is unable to hold itself back at this boundary, letting its desires become too strong, the forming of an aesthetic judgement is impaired. Whenever the cool, cognitive judgement prevails, the sense of beauty is killed. The forming of an aesthetic judgement may also be seen as a continual meeting between individual and world, or individual and another human. The decisive factor is an *artistic* satisfaction. In the learning process the feeling barrier plays the main part; it can be transformed by the learning path.

14.3. Forming a Moral Judgement

From a psychological point of view, moral judgement and cognitive judgement are opposites. The judging soul has to give up its outer search for truth to be able, independently, to find the inner moral truth. Thereby, the experiencing soul becomes an inwardly communicating soul; the world capitulates in the face of the inner spiritual truth. Here, the opponent in the learning process is the will barrier. It is overcome by learning to form moral judgements. It has become repeatedly obvious in adult education that to include all three faculties considerably promotes the independence of people's judgement. Conversely, the one-sided emphasis of one of the three faculties causes unhealthy side effects. Also, it can be observed that the three support each other. Many people searching for the truth have realized how much they can discover through artistic activity. Artists have found that their way of experiencing art has been deepened by an attitude of questioning and research. Moreover, in adult education each Learning Step has three aspects: an *understanding* component, an *experiential* one, and one that gives *meaning*. None of the three must be neglected. Encouraging people's independent judgement in this threefold way may become a catalyst for the learning process. In particular, in the context of 'Learning how to Learn', a large amount of time and space should be allowed for this.

The scientist strives to investigate the reality behind the phenomena. The artist, on the other hand, tries to express this reality in this world in an artistic way. This in itself shows how essential the marriage of science and art is. No genuine spiritual research without artistic activity; no new art without spiritual research. The strict separation of the two that exists in educational institutions has been going on for long enough. Both science and art have been seriously impeded by it in their development. Where this separation is maintained in training courses, the participants are developed in a one-sided way, and the foundations for a later professional deformation are laid. In an age where people are decisively determined by technology, this is an imperative necessity. The head-bound scientist and the unworldly artist are phenomena that could be healed in adult education courses from the outset.

The contribution that art is making to our culture, while humanity is crossing the threshold towards recognizing the supersensible, will take many different forms in the future, and will play a part in all aspects of life. Already today, we have:

— Art as therapy;
— Social art; not yet being fully practically applied, but as a field of art in its own right which is in the process of being discovered and worked with;
— Art as a means of promoting learning processes;
— Art in professional work, etc.

For further details on this aspect, see Appendix I.

14.4. Didactic Aspects

In many courses, adult educators have discovered the possibilities inherent in painting a picture together, making a poem together or creating a drama, doing modelling or improvising music, designing buildings. These are attempts to involve the mutual destiny forces of the participants in the creation of something. For the learning process, the point is not to create a piece of art, but to awaken creative forces in the soul of the person who is practising and who is perceiving.

15. Adult Educators: Their Education and Their Path

The main task of adult education is to awaken the will to learn. The basic question of the adult educator, therefore, must be: How can I awaken the will in the other person? Awakening the will means awakening the *three drives* in us. These drives are always there, but usually dormant. Only our ego can awaken them. It is not possible to awaken something in us from the outside, least of all the will. All that can be done is create an opportunity, a stimulus, a challenge, that will allow a kind of self-awakening to occur. This is a chief task of the adult educator. Ultimately, however, it takes place through the self-engendered inner activity of the learner. Self-awakening might also be called 'Learning how to Learn'. In other words, the real task of the adult educator is to teach adults the activity of 'self-learning'. What gifts are needed for this purpose? To discover and develop these, the adult educator has to go on a path of discovery, or rather, of Spiritual Research.

15.1. The Learning Event

To start on this path, whenever insight occurs, whenever an important event takes place, or we achieve something fruitful, we need consciously to ask ourselves: '*What* is it that I have learned here?' We must then try to put the answer, when found, into words, so that it does not get lost. This means we are really doing a kind of learning review. It gives us the basis we need for researching the path we have been on, to arrive at this particular learning event.

15.2. The Learning Path

This path is often hidden, is a mysterious process. An observation, a conversation, a book, a walk, an illness, even an accident, may contribute to it. The learning path has a biography, and this biography needs to be understood. Biographical research into *our* learning path will develop the gifts in us to awaken 'Learning how to Learn' (including the biography of the learning path) in the other person. In other words, it is necessary to become clear about the *learning event* first, then to become familiar with our own *path*. This must then be transformed into practical teaching forms.

15.3. Creating a Learning Situation

As a next step, this self-examination needs therefore to be made fruitful for other people. In our learning biography we will discover certain basic elements that together have reforged a large number of experiences into an ability. These basic elements have become the material with the help of which learning situations may be created—often in a very simplified way. The core of the adult educator's arduous, long learning biography becomes a concrete and operational learning possibility for others.

Thus, many exercises have come about which are often very simple but which have a strong effect, because they are densified experiences. Many lectures are nothing but the communication of knowledge by lecturers who have not taken the trouble to go through these three steps asking themselves:

— How and what was my learning moment?
— What is the learning path I have gone through for this to happen?
— How can the essential aspect of this path be made fruitful for others?

Following this path, our lectures will assume a different character—there will be less communication of knowledge, but more awakening of the will. Our aim is the latter, which, however, we can achieve only if we embark on this research path. Thereby we turn ourselves into adult educators. The numerous excellent artists, scientists and specialists will become adult educators *only* if they have first made their own development an instrument for others. Also, of course, the drive to acquire knowledge and insight, the drive to develop, and the drive to improve, need constantly to be reawakened, otherwise it is not possible to awaken them in others. All the numerous individual exercises that allow this path to grow into a faculty will not be listed here. According to our situation and need it will certainly be possible to create them ourselves.

15.4. The Working Together of the Adult Education Group

This book has tried to make it clear that a productive and creative process among a carrying group, staff group or faculty, is the prerequisite for designing and implementing courses. Usually, what individuals can offer is inadequate, since their capacities arise out of fundamentally different professional backgrounds. This is why we have to learn to work together with colleagues who are each very different. As a great deal has been published about co-operation in groups, this will not be gone into in detail here. Only what is specific to a faculty group will be emphasized.

— Good adult educators love their subject, but do they perhaps love it more than their task as adult educators? This would lead to numerous inner and outer conflicts in teaching situations. A genuine working together between staff members is possible only when the course participants are the centre of attention, are the connecting, decisive element. For many specialists, it is often a painful sacrifice to regard their beloved teaching subject as something that is serving the process of another adult human being's developing and learning. If we succeed in achieving this attitude, we will discover that the other subjects also serve, and that only all colleagues together will be able to cater for the whole human being. This does not mean, however, that the necessity has gone for stepping out of the teaching situation at regular intervals to be able fully to devote ourselves again to our own subject.

— Something very important may arise out of the creative teamwork among the adult educators: namely a deepening of this new profession as such. Because humanity will have an ever increasing need for adult education, this book approaches that discipline as a profession in its own right, as something with an immensely important future. The three paths of learning (see Chapter 3), point the way to this future. Already early in this century, Jean Piaget declared that education is '*éducation permanente*' that stops only at death. Since the subject-disciplines are so different, there is the possibility of overcoming our one-sidedness through working together as colleagues. At the same time, the didactic possibilities of the other subjects are discovered. In this way, working together becomes a possibility for personal development.

— All adult educators are in danger of not only becoming 'subject blind' but also of getting stuck in their style of teaching. The best means of breaking out of this prison is to enlist the support of trusted colleagues. They can give important hints. Thereby, collegial relationships become a mutually continuous path of development. The author has to admit that his path was guided mainly by colleagues and participants.

— A further aspect of work among colleagues is co-operative research. This new profession is a young one; it is only just beginning. Innumerable aspects of what is really happening in adult education are still to be discovered. Already we know quite an amount about children. This is due particularly to the vastly developing and spreading Steiner Waldorf Education Movement. About adult education, however, we know very little as yet. Numerous methods, elements and means of learning are still to be found, as well as innumerable didactic methods. More and more research is needed into what modern human beings are really going through inwardly as they cross over the threshold. The needs must be recognized, and the appropriate answers must be found. Since this transformation of humanity is a continual one, every answer soon becomes obsolete. Many educational institutions are lagging behind, employing learning models that were used by the previous generation. The only solution lies in the group of colleagues continually questioning and researching, thereby constantly renewing our educational institutions. This means that the profession of 'adult educator' requires that the educators themselves should be both *teachers* awakening the will of their course participants, and *researchers* creatively working together with each other.

The following Chapter gives a few further indications about the hygiene of the Adult Learning Process. Having significant 'helping conversations' with participants seems to be one of the main elements in this respect.

16. The Hygienic Element in Adult Learning

A common attitude is that in the educational system students learn and are taught, while the personal element, the students' mental, emotional and physical well-being is their own business. The faculty is supposed to leave the students completely free, because all the above-mentioned is their own responsibility, is not part of the responsibilities of the teachers. This requires the following replies, as already indicated in other chapters of this book:

— Firstly, that many participants are already damaged by their environment, culture or education when they enter the course;
— Secondly, that during an effective, serious learning process, many dormant and undigested inner problems will rise to the surface;
— Thirdly, that the teaching itself may have a one-sided, damaging or destructive effect.
— Fourthly, that in our time and age, all people are in a threshold situation—more or less consciously—in which sense-perceptible and supersensible elements play into each other in a confusing way.

This means that the old attitude cannot be maintained any longer; rather, the learning situation demands personal assistance and shared responsibility. What is meant here, is a 'normal' hygienic element, not extreme situations that need psychotherapeutic care and which must be left to the specialists. How, then, can this hygienic element be taken care of?

16.1. Hygienic Elements in Teaching

All learning processes and programmes need to be aimed at wholeness and balance. The total human being needs to be addressed, for everything that is one-sided, overemphasized, or routine has a damaging effect. What is essential for hygiene is a rhythmical way of proceeding, for this involves one of the most important healing forces for individuals and society. If participants get acquainted with this, and practise during their learning process and learn how to use it, much has been achieved. It is not necessary to say much more about this, here, since this book has already given numerous indications about the striving for wholeness, balance and rhythm. The Sevenfold Learning Process in itself can become a healing process.

16.2. Personal Support

What many educational institutions try to do for this purpose is to offer what are often called 'helping conversations'. This conversation between teacher and participant is not meant to be therapy or treatment, and even less so a dependent relationship between the adult participant and one of the staff. The two meet each other as grown up, independent people, who counsel *each other* in a helpful and supportive way that seeks to deepen their mutual understanding. This is why it is called the 'helping conversation'. At nearly all educational institutions, students complain about how difficult it is to find somebody to have a conversation with, about personal experiences or questions they have on their minds and that seem outwardly to have little to do with the subject being studied. The staff are often under too great a strain, have little time, and are busy with other things. Often, the most important inner experiences of the participants are not given sufficient attention, and consequently find a destructive outlet elsewhere.

The goal of this conversational hygiene can be easily described. However, practice has often shown that neither the staff nor the participants are expert at this art of conversation from the start. People need to be educated in the art of the 'helping conversation', and this should therefore be part of the adult educator's professional accomplishments.

One advantage of having developed this art is that we get to know ourselves much better. Soon we discover that, during the conversation, we get in our own way, and how we affect others unwittingly. 'Helping' does not mean that the conversations are superficial—quite the contrary. They can be very deep and moving; however, it remains an activity of *mutual* exploration, with both partners in the conversation fully maintaining their personal independence and responsibility. There are courses on how to lead a 'helping conversation', giving many approaches that need to be further developed by the participants themselves.

Since the problems are often connected with 'threshold', or 'inner crisis' phenomena, an important component of the conversation is that we should have experience and knowledge of these phenomena. Therefore, the spiritual-scientific literature that deals with these aspects should be studied thoroughly.

All this indicates that helping conversations are an obligatory component in the hygiene of the learning process.

16.3. Inner and Outer 'Hygiene' in the Adult Educator's Work

Adult educators are, in this profession, mainly focused on other people. They are being challenged in every aspect of their thinking, feeling and behaviour by participants and colleagues. This means that they are continuously being drawn outwards and therefore become mainly outer-directed. As a consequence, there is the danger that their own inner life will not be cared for and nourished sufficiently. This leads to an inner emptiness that will ultimately create an unhygienic situation that consumes the life-forces. With the symptoms of so-called 'burn-out', they have to take certain hygienic counter-measures to care for their own inner hygiene as well. These include: regularly spending time on their own; learning to cope with being alone with themselves; to a certain extent, in these moments, leaving behind the never-ending problems of the participants.

Often, adult educators become 'workaholics' because they can hardly bear to be confronted with themselves in their alone moments. Let us not forget that this profession is burdened with much that needs digesting. Therefore, the personal work hygiene demands rhythmically planned moments in which adult educators may totally switch off, recover and recharge their used-up life-forces. How this is done, and how often, varies with individuals. It does need to be done from the start, however. These quieter moments may also serve to deepen, through personal experience, understanding of the current threshold situation. This self-research is a good schooling to help adult educators be able to accompany the participants with information, advice and support. A rhythmical alternation between inner and outer activity is necessary for the hygiene of this adult education profession.

The aspect of a hygienic organization of the environment will not be dealt with here, because extensive literature is already available on this subject. Naturally, colour, design, decoration, etc. of the rooms will have an influence, but not as strongly as with children. Noises are also distracting; on the other hand, however, modern people have become used to noise to such an extent that complete quiet may even be experienced as frightening.

17. Examples of Practical Applications

17.1. The Learning Group

In various institutions, successful attempts have already been made to deepen the first four steps of the Sevenfold Learning Process by means of group work. Introducing this attempt is not too difficult, although accompanying these group processes does take some experience.

— The participants are divided into groups of from five to eight persons, with one facilitator for each group.
— Everyone listens to a lecture that is being presented, then the groups get together to assimilate what they have just heard. This takes place in four steps, essentially following the first four steps of the learning process. The exercise can be done every day after the lecture, with, time permitting, a further step being added every day. Usually by the third or fourth day the participants are able to perform all four steps successively. The steps may be described in the following way:

First day (Step 1): What did he or she say? What did we hear? *The group as a whole* recreates the presentation (without adding points of view; *process of breathing in and out*).

Second day (Steps 1 and 2): What were the essential learning moments *for me* (choose one or two), and how did I experience them? (*Relating to the subject, warming*). The group shares these learning moments and emotional experiences without discussing them.

Third day (Steps 1, 2, and 3): Now, the essential points are *worked through, deepened, compared, evaluated.* The group tries to distinguish the essential from the inessential, entering into a lively discussion. (*Process of assimilating and digesting.*)

Fourth day (Steps 1 through 4): What *new* questions, thoughts, feelings or intentions does this whole process awaken *in me*? (After five minutes of silence and concentration, everyone writes down their findings.) The new questions are shared in the group; again, without judging or discussing them. (*Individualizing of the learning process.*)

Every Learning Step is explained before being applied. In the First Step the group facilitator may make the participants aware of the fact that this joint repetition enriches and deepens what they have heard. As a side-effect, they will listen better the following day, so that less is lost. Also, the discipline to hold back judgements and responses while taking in is extremely important.

About the Second Step, we should take into consideration that it involves a far more personal and subjective element. Everyone has experienced the situation in a very different way, and it becomes obvious how the content of the lecture merges with what people have experienced in the past. Often, as a side-effect, some self-knowledge occurs.

The Third Step leads to the actual group discussion. Opinions and judgements are confronted, which prepares the participants for developing totally new points of view. Here, the facilitator has to make sure that this step does not go on for ever, yet offers enough assimilation for the next step to be tried.

The Fourth Step begins with an interval, during which people become quiet, inwardly taking a step back to allow what is new to rise up in them. What is important, is to experience this as something truly new for oneself. Likewise it is important that the members of the group should respect it as such. This group exercise has the following advantages:

— The participants learn to understand and improve their learning processes, and in the long run become able to use them for themselves as well.

— They discover that well-guided group work may considerably contribute to their learning.

— Also, for a lecturer who may be sitting in listening passively, this may be a wonderful learning process! They often hear for the first time how their lecture has affected the participants and what they do with it. Anyway, in the author's case it meant gaining healthy self-knowledge.

17.2. The 'Landscape Procedure'

A teacher known to the author shared the following thoughts: Each participant has within themselves an 'inner landscape', composed of all their learning and life experiences. The landscape shows innumerable variations of individual parts, colours, weather qualities, hills, valleys, etc. and yet it is a totality because it is all living within one individual. If the teacher now introduces something completely new into this landscape, such as archetypal pictures from spiritual science or new images of the human being, this may considerably upset the delicately balanced landscape. Storms, volcanic eruptions, high and low pressure areas, or what have you, may result. The teacher who has decided to accompany these happenings as a learning process, might continue as follows:

1. After a preparatory phase, each of the participants describes as well as possible what their inner landscape really looks like, how they find their way around in it, and what questions are living in them about it. The participants experience the description of what is in them as a kind of breathing-in, whereas it becomes a kind of breathing-out when described in relation to others. Obviously, artistic approaches could be used here as well.

2. The tutor then introduces a number of new concepts that need to find their place in the 'landscape'. The confrontation of old and new elements triggers off a warmth process. The conscious friction between old and new has an igniting effect.

3. Next, each of the participants writes a paper describing what happened in the Second Step, and what it all means to them—a questioning, critical, evaluating observation. The paper is given to the tutor who adds his or her comments. For the participants, this step means digesting and assimilating.

4. The papers are then discussed thoroughly in groups of five participants. In doing so all of them together should try to find new points of view. These discussions are experienced by the participants as a critical point in the learning process.

5. Then each of the participants has to investigate in themselves the consequences of this discussion and decide what their next step should be. They make a decision about their next Learning Step, discussing it with their tutor.

6. The participants put their decision into practice.

7. In the end, they evaluate thoroughly together what they have learnt; in doing so many new points of view are likely to arise. What is striking in this process is the alternation between individual work, group work and contributions by the tutor. The 'landscape' picture in the beginning creates a very different process; moreover, the emphasis on 'Learning how to Learn' is characteristic. This shows that many other variations of this Sevenfold Learning Process can be imagined.

See Appendix II for details of how one institution worked with this.

18. Concluding Remarks

Behind the usual way of imparting knowledge and training practical skills, on the one hand, and what has been attempted in this book, on the other, a real spiritual battle is hiding. In the majority of our educational institutions young people are forced to receive undigested, uncomprehended knowledge and information into their personalities, believing that it is real and true. An exceptional amount of pragmatically oriented exercising is prescribed, and the students do not even become aware of the extent to which they are being conditioned. Whoever works much with students knows how much subliminal hatred is in them against the university system, since no, or very little, attention is paid to the human quality living in them. A healthy adult education should therefore always take as its starting point this very human part of our being, 'the middle sphere'; only then can the two poles of knowledge and skills be humanized. This however, is an altogether different conception of Adult Learning Processes. Learning then means to change, to transform, to develop; indeed, to become increasingly human.

The other approach regards the human being approximately as an instrument that is to be trained. Instrument for what? Instrument for whom? A look ahead into the future seems appropriate at the end of this book. The underlying needs of this world will increase more and more. Ideas for answering and meeting these needs must and will be found. However, there will be ever fewer people who possess the faculties to realize the answers and truly meet these questions. For the progress that can be made in the future will depend on the human being. New solutions require new faculties. This means that adult education holds the key to the future in its hand. The twentieth century has brought us a new approach to child education. However, here, too, it becomes obvious that its further development depends on appropriately developed teachers of whom new faculties are required.

The twenty-first century will demand a new, up-to-date, adult education, otherwise there will be no true progress. All technology will more and more depend on how it is used by humanity. Besides the problems of the world there are the problems of people, which will also increase more and more. As already indicated in this book, the human soul is threatened to such an extent that it is no longer possible, at an inner and an outer level, to meet the demands of life without an inner spiritual schooling. Therefore, already today, learning without a spiritual schooling is no longer sufficient. This shows that in the next century a lifelong adult education for everybody will be in demand. Consequently, adult education will become the bottleneck for a wholesome progress of the human being and humanity. This book is an attempt at a first step of creating a new basis for adult education as a profession in its own right. May this first step be followed by many more.

A fundamental starting point is the synthesis of the three learning paths described in Chapter 3. Learning *for* life, learning *through* life, and learning to live *in* the reality of the spiritual world is not a question of making them happen one after the other, or at the same time. The point is that, from the start, these three paths should help to create a new adult education that represents the university of the future.

In times long past the places of learning were called mystery schools, to which people travelled from afar, and some of which are still known today. There, however, the unity of the Three Learning Paths was based upon completely different conditions. The last school still possessing a faint reflection of this was the School of Chartres, where the Seven Liberal Arts together made a kind of initiation path possible. (See Chapter 6.) The university of the future will again have to respect the dignity of human beings in their knowledge and faculties; however in a totally new way. Learning for Life, Learning through the Forces of Destiny, and Spiritual Schooling will interpenetrate and be mutually stimulating and enriching. However, to achieve this purpose the human will to go this way in particular needs to be awakened: the free will which in our technological culture is being weakened more and more. Our knowledge is a result, but the youthful will still has its future ahead. What is required is an adult education enabling our ego to awaken this will; in other words: Adult Education as an Awakening of the Will!

Appendix I:
Notes on Art as a Medium for Adult Learning

By Marlies Rainer: Alanus School of Art, Alfter, Germany

This Appendix consists of notes on how art may be used in various developmental processes. Although far from complete, it is included to give an idea of what is now being explored in different fields.

Traditionally, the arts have been shown in exhibitions and performances as different creative forms by accomplished artists. The artist works with changing and focusing materials, words, music or movement in a creative process so that the spirit starts to live in it. At the same time, the artist goes through an inward process of change.

It has been recognized that these moving and enlivening forces that are experienced in the artistic process can become effective in any human being. Thus art is becoming more and more a medium through which processes for human development may be explored; in this case, Adult Learning Processes. In addition to courses which develop creative potential through an artistic training, there are also some interesting approaches to letting art serve specifically the educational process and learning situations. These processes can develop a creative capacity that is applicable to social or work situations, and, in the latter, a greater awareness of what is manifesting in the situation.

For example, a problematic work situation is experienced in a different way through art, by experiencing the 'gesture' of the situation in a picture. In the process of creating the picture, by feeling into the dynamics and qualities of the situation, the situation is then clarified. The people involved more and more develop the ability to deal with the issue because they have experienced it in a transformative way. The picture produced is less important than the process itself, hence no artistic talent is required. Everyone can do it!

The exercise of entering into painting, modelling, music, poetry, speech, drama or eurythmy, can affect people positively when hardened situations can be solved (softened) and inflammatory situations calmed down (cooled). It affects both health and life attitudes.

Another potential for working with art is the development of specific faculties, such as:

— Widened and deepened ability to perceive;
— Empathy;
— Courage to judge out of the whole situation, instead of from just one side;
— Courage to enter into an open process;
— Decisiveness, etc., etc.

Using art to support development is, of course, not new. For example, involving the students in art plays an important part in Waldorf (or Steiner) Education, where it serves the development of the child in many different ways. Art therapy supports the healing process by strengthening the forces of the individual who is struggling with some physical or psychological problem.

In the application to adult education, exercises are being developed which support the Seven Steps of the Adult Learning Process.

The following table indicates various ways in which art can serve in adult education.

TYPE	AIM	EFFECT
Work of Art	To express and reveal something	Touches the observer
'Hygienic compensation'	To balance one-sided demands	Harmonizes the whole person
Picture of a situation	To make conscious and show the 'gesture' of a situation	Developing awareness of the essential issue
Educational	To develop personally	The development of certain faculties, for example: perception; flexibility; courage; perseverance; decisiveness, etc.
Therapeutic	To support healing processes	Strengthens the healing forces
Social Art	To arrange one's whole daily life and professional situation in an artistic way	The art becomes educational, healing, creative

Appendix II:
A Learning-to-Learn Weekend for Future Steiner Waldorf Teachers

By Robert Hell: Munich Institute for Steiner Waldorf Education

The Munich Institute for Steiner Waldorf Education (founded in 1990) offers a three-year course for already-trained teachers. The first two years are part-time, and the third year consists of practical work experience in one of the South Bavarian Steiner Waldorf Schools.

The staff felt that the course, which is offered by practising teachers, ought to be more firmly based on the principles of *adult* education. They twice invited Coen van Houten to run training sessions in that area. What he offered was designed for the course leaders, who were to learn not only about adult education, but also about their own learning potentials and blocks! After these two sessions, which were a year apart, the faculty decided to organize their own 'Learning-to-Learn' weekend workshop for their course participants. What follows is an account of this.

To offer, without outside help, a Learning-to-Learn weekend to all 80 participants in 1994, required some courage on the part of the staff. It meant a large step forward in the development of the young Institute.

The programme ran as follows:

Friday: Introduction and talk on basic concepts of adult education.

Learning Groups.

Saturday: Artistic introduction—walking and mirroring a partner's walk; exercising with tones, both to practise listening, and to enhance the group process.

Talk on the learning process.

Making a learning diagnosis:
a. Individually;
b. Sharing in Small Groups.

Sharing experiences ('harvesting') in a plenary session.

Separate meetings of three course groups to prepare the year's work.

(Somewhere in all this there were breaks and meals!)

Comments:
Before the participants were formally welcomed, they were reminded that each human encounter is a challenge because it bears in it the fundamental risk of failure. This could be lessened only by a serious attempt to listen actively!

The Course Facilitator then led the audience members back into their individual learning biographies: first experiences at school, university and adult courses, etc., emphasizing the experiences they had had in class, with the teachers, activities, smells, visual impressions, etc. He then stood up and walked up and down, like a 'typical' teacher, suggesting that he might ask people a few questions! This was to demonstrate that we are deeply marked for life in our learning habits and roles by these early experiences.

The Facilitator then pointed out that for adults it was their ego that served as their teacher and that, therefore, it was their personal responsibility as to what and how they learned—even at that very moment while he was talking— and that out of this responsibility they were called upon to contribute to the work of the course in which they were studying. The learning would take place on three different levels:

a. On the Institute level, concerning Anthroposophy and Steiner/Waldorf pedagogy;
b. On the biographical level, concerning their life situation, their motives for becoming Steiner Waldorf teachers;

c. On the spiritual level, where schooling would be encouraged.

The Participants

Where and when did learning take place? Had we ever come to a point where we realized that our old skills and competencies were failing, and where new abilities were necessary? These are crisis points of understanding, of developing and in being active in the learning process. But, how could we adults awaken our will to learn? In the learning groups, in each of which was an observer to help co-ordinate the discussion, participants were given the following four tasks to be worked through in order:

a. Reconstruct what you have perceived of the talk without using your notes. Refrain from making any personal comments;
b. State, individually, what was difficult/easy, pleasant/unpleasant, important, etc. for you, without discussion;
c. Discuss the talk freely and critically, starting from your personal relationship to it. What was/was not important, contradictory, etc.?
d. After a five-minute pause, come to a statement as to what personal question/information/insight, etc. you are left with. Do not discuss.

After an artistic introduction, the Saturday morning was started by the observers reporting back from the learning groups. This step had three functions:

a. The participants could reflect on how they had dealt with the tasks;
b. The reports revealed how the talk had been received, and offered much material concerning learning blocks;
c. Everyone had experienced the first four steps of the learning process before it was presented as a whole. The learning process was then illustrated in three different ways:

— As a series of steps building on each other;

- As a guide to discovering our possible learning blocks (there were numerous examples given);
— Different types of task as examples (sailing, learning to take responsibility, etc.)

In question time, there was a brief discussion in which the complexity of the learning process was clarified. The individual learning diagnosis was then a logical consequence of the discussion.

In the final plenum, the participants were asked to share their experiences concerning the qualities of encounter in the weekend, including the artistic introduction.

General Review. Friday night was an unexpected experience for most participants. They had been surprised, or even angry, that they had to *do* something. Being confronted with early school memories, and/or the Facilitator getting up and pretending to act like a teacher, was so strong an emotional experience for many that they were not open to what they called the 'theory'. They would have liked to have had more time to dwell on that experience. Some were disconcerted by a Facilitator who refused to play the expected role (and said so!). For some learning groups, instructions were a problem. They felt they did not have enough material to digest. Many others, however, were enthralled by the evening. They regarded the learning groups as a rich and deep experience.

Saturday Morning Review. Overnight, many of the problems seemed to have dissolved. They could be regarded and understood as barriers in the learning process. In the discussion on the learning process, still with all the participants, the very personal and constructive contributions showed that all (staff and students) had made a noticeable move towards learning together. Biographical learning, or the individual learning biography, had become the crucial issue.

We decided to come back to the issue at various times over the following year to explore more fully the question: How can we overcome our learning blocks?

Notes

1. Rudolf Steiner, 'Hochschule und öffentliches Leben', in: *Gesammelte Aufsätze zur Kultur- und Zeitgeschichte 1887–1901*, GA 31, p. 301 ff, Rudolf Steiner Verlag, 1966. [Not published in English.]
2. Lecture of 18 January 1909, in *Anthroposophy in Everyday Life*, Anthroposophic Press, 1995.
3. F.W. Zeylmans van Emmichoven, *The Anthroposophical Understanding of the Human Soul*, Anthroposophic Press, 1982.
4. Rudolf Steiner, *The Riddle of Humanity*, Rudolf Steiner Press, 1990.
5. Ibid., p. 87–91. Although the quotation is from this volume, a few amendments have been made. The language has been made non-gender specific; a translation error has been corrected (in the English edition, the last word of the quotation is given as *macrocosm*; it should be *microcosm*); the paragraphing has been altered slightly.
6. Christof Lindenau, *Der übende Mensch. Anthroposophie-Studium als Ausgangspunkt moderner Geistesschulung*, Verlag Freies Geistesleben, 1983. [Not published in English.]
7. See, for example, Rudolf Steiner, *Guidance in Esoteric Training*, Rudolf Steiner Press, 1994.
8. Bernard Lievegoed, *Schulungswege. Der Weg des einzelnen und der Weg in karmischer Gemeinschaft*, Verlag am Goetheanum, 1992. [Not published in English.]
   Together with: Rudolf Steiner, *True and False Paths in Spiritual Investigation*, Rudolf Steiner Press and Anthroposophic Press, 1985.
9. As, for example: Bernard Lievegoed, *Phases, The Spiritual Rhythms in Adult Life*, Rudolf Steiner Press, 1997.
10. See also Rudolf Steiner, *Karmic Relationships*, Vol. 2., Rudolf Steiner Press, 1974.
11. See Note 3.

Bibliography

Johann Valentin Andreae, 'The Chymical Wedding of Christian Rosenkreutz', included in: Paul M. Allen, compiler and editor, *A Christian Rosenkreutz Anthology*, Rudolf Steiner Publications, 1981.

Thomas Göbel, *Die Quellen der Kunst. Lebendige Sinne und Phantasie als Schlüssel zur Architektur*, Verlag am Goetheanum, 1981. [Not published in English.]

Christof Lindenau, *Der übende Mensch. Anthroposophie-Studium als Ausgangspunkt moderner Geistesschulung*, 2nd. edition, Verlag Freies Geistesleben, 1983. [Not published in English.]

Yehudi Menuhin, *Kunst und Wissenschaft als verwandte Begriffe. Versuch einer vergleichenden Anatomie ihrer Erscheinungswesen in verschiedenen Bereichen menschlichen Strebens*, Frankfurt/M, 1960.

Jörgen Smit. *Der Ausbildungsalltag als Herausforderung*, Verlag am Goetheanum, 1989. [Not published in English.]

Rudolf Steiner, *Anthroposophy (A Fragment)*, Anthroposophic Press, 1996.

Rudolf Steiner, *Gesammelte Aufsätze zur Kultur- und Zeitgeschichte 1887–1901*. 2nd. edition, Rudolf Steiner Verlag, 1987. [Not published in English.]

Rudolf Steiner, *Course for Young Doctors*, Mercury Press, 1994.

Rudolf Steiner, *The Reappearance of Christ in the Etheric*, Anthroposophic Press, 1983.

Rudolf Steiner, *The Riddle of Humanity*, Rudolf Steiner Press, 1990.

Rudolf Steiner, *True and False Paths in Spiritual Investigation*, Rudolf Steiner Press and Anthroposophic Press, 1985.

Matthias Wais, *Biographiearbeit und Lebensberatung*, Verlag Urachhaus, 1992. [Not published in English.]

F.W. Zeylmans van Emmichoven, *The Anthroposophical Understanding of the Human Soul*, Anthroposophic Press, 1982.